True Stories of
Teens in the Holocaust

ESCAPE—
TEENS
ON THE RUN

PRIMARY
SOURCES
FROM THE
HOLOCAUST

Other Titles in the
True Stories of
Teens in the Holocaust
Series

COURAGEOUS TEEN RESISTERS
PRIMARY SOURCES FROM THE HOLOCAUST
ISBN-13: 978-0-7660-3269-9

HIDDEN TEENS,
HIDDEN LIVES
PRIMARY SOURCES FROM THE HOLOCAUST
ISBN-13: 978-0-7660-3271-2

SHATTERED YOUTH
IN NAZI GERMANY
PRIMARY SOURCES FROM THE HOLOCAUST
ISBN-13: 978-0-7660-3268-2

TRAPPED—YOUTH IN THE
NAZI GHETTOS
PRIMARY SOURCES FROM THE HOLOCAUST
ISBN-13: 978-0-7660-3272-9

YOUTH DESTROYED—THE NAZI CAMPS
PRIMARY SOURCES FROM THE HOLOCAUST
ISBN-13: 978-0-7660-3273-6

True Stories of
Teens in the Holocaust

ESCAPE— TEENS ON THE RUN

PRIMARY SOURCES FROM THE HOLOCAUST

Linda Jacobs Altman

Holocaust research by
Margaret Shannon,
Senior Research Historian,
Washington Historical Research

Enslow Publishers, Inc.
40 Industrial Road
Box 398
Berkeley Heights, NJ 07922
USA
http://www.enslow.com

Library of Congress Cataloging-in-Publication Data

Altman, Linda Jacobs, 1943–
    Escape, teens on the run : primary sources from the Holocaust / Linda Jacobs Altman.
        p. cm. — (True stories of teens in the Holocaust)
    Summary: "Discusses children and teens on the run during the Holocaust in Europe, including the different ways young people escaped the Nazis, places of refuge in Europe, and hiding and resistance"—Provided by publisher.
    Includes bibliographical references and index.
    ISBN-13: 978-0-7660-3270-5
    ISBN-10: 0-7660-3270-1
    1. Jewish children in the Holocaust—Juvenile literature. 2. Jewish teenagers—Europe—History—20th century—Juvenile literature. 3. Unaccompanied refugee children—Europe—History—20th century—Juvenile literature. 4. Escapes—Europe—History—20th century—Juvenile literature. 5. Government, Resistance to—Europe—History—20th century—Juvenile literature. 6. World War, 1939–1945—Children—Juvenile literature. 7. World War, 1939–1945—Refugees—Juvenile literature. 8. Holocaust, Jewish (1939–1945)—Juvenile literature. 9. Holocaust, Jewish (1939–1945)—Sources—Juvenile literature. I. Title.
    D804.48.A48 2010
    940.53'180835—dc22   2009021378

Printed in the United States of America

112009 Lake Book Manufacturing, Inc., Melrose Park, IL

10 9 8 7 6 5 4 3 2 1

To Our Readers: We have done our best to make sure all Internet Addresses in this book were active and appropriate when we went to press. However, the author and the publisher have no control over and assume no liability for the material available on those Internet sites or on other Web sites they may link to. Any comments or suggestions can be sent by e-mail to comments@enslow.com or to the address on the back cover.

✪ Enslow Publishers, Inc., is committed to printing our books on recycled paper. The paper in every book contains 10% to 30% post-consumer waste (PCW). The cover board on the outside of each book contains 100% PCW. Our goal is to do our part to help young people and the environment too!

Every effort has been made to locate all copyright holders of material used in this book. If any errors or omissions have occurred, please contact us at www.enslow.com. We will try to make corrections in future editions.

Illustration Credits: Enslow Publishers, Inc., p. 72; USHMM, courtesy of Alfred Brosan, p. 88; USHMM, courtesy of Alice Lev, p. 26; USHMM, courtesy of Betty Troper Yaeger, p. 69; USHMM, courtesy of Bruna D'Urbino, pp. 104–105; USHMM, courtesy of Charlene Schiff, pp. 28, 116; USHMM, courtesy of Charles Martin Roman, pp. 101, 117; USHMM, courtesy of Herbert and Vera Karliner, p. 64; USHMM, courtesy of Huroki Sugihara, p. 48; USHMM, courtesy of Inge Engelhard Sadan, pp. 1, 3, 55; USHMM, courtesy of Instytut Pamieci Narodowej, p. 51; USHMM, courtesy of Johanna Neumann, pp. 92, 117; USHMM, courtesy of Leo Melamed, pp. 34, 36; USHMM, courtesy of Liane Reif-Lehrer, pp. 18, 116; USHMM, courtesy of Library of Congress, p. 10; USHMM, courtesy of Lucile Szepsenwol Camhi, pp. 46, 116; USHMM, courtesy of Mark Chrzanowski, p. 112; USHMM, courtesy of Martin Smith, pp. 24–25; USHMM, courtesy of National Archives and Records Administration, pp. 13, 39, 67, 116; USHMM, courtesy of Norbert Swislocki, p. 90; USHMM, courtesy of Peter Kollisch, pp. 59, 117; USHMM, courtesy of Ruth Berkowicz Segal, pp. 80, 82; USHMM, courtesy of Samuel and Ala Brand, p. 110; USHMM, courtesy of Trudy Isenberg, p. 21; USHMM, courtesy of Ursula Sligmann Lowenstein, p. 43; USHMM, courtesy of Vitka Kempner Kovner, p. 96; USHMM, courtesy of Walter Karliner, pp. 74, 117; USHMM, courtesy of YIVO Institute, p. 98.

Cover Illustration: USHMM, courtesy of Inge Engelhard Sadan (Photo of Inge Engelhard from her children's identification card issued to her by the German police that revoked her citizenship. She used this card instead of a passport to go to England on a Kindertransport where she survived the war).

Contents

Acknowledgments 6

Chapter 1 **Alicia's Journey** 7

Chapter 2 **The Right Time to Go** 16

Chapter 3 **The Search for Refuge** 31

Chapter 4 **Two Journeys** 50

Chapter 5 **One Step Ahead of Disaster** 71

Chapter 6 **Fighting Back** 95

Chapter 7 **Luck and Survival** 109

Timeline 116

Chapter Notes 118

Glossary 123

Further Reading 124

Internet Addresses 125

Index 126

Acknowledgments

Special thanks to the people of the United States Holocaust Memorial Museum in Washington, D.C., for all their help in completing this book.

Chapter One

ALICIA'S JOURNEY

Alicia Jurman was eleven years old when Germany invaded eastern Poland. In the city of Buczacz, Jews watched in silent horror as the Nazis came into town. Years later, one image stuck in Alicia's mind: "Mostly I remember the motorcycles. To this day I shudder when I hear the roaring sound of a motorcycle outside my house. No one really knew what would happen, and everyone was in shock."[1]

The Sound of Thunder

In a matter of days, the Germans called for Jewish men between the ages of eighteen and fifty to register at the police station. Alicia's father reported as ordered, expecting to be home by lunchtime. Around two o'clock, the family heard a distant noise. It rumbled, it cracked, it stopped and started throughout the afternoon. *Thunder*, Alicia thought. It had to be thunder.

After three days with no word, Alicia's brother Zachary remembered that odd noise: maybe it was not thunder at all. Maybe it was something much worse than thunder. When Alicia realized what her brother meant, she flew into a wild rage. "It *was* thunder!" she screamed, and set out to prove her point: "I ran over the [meadow] and into the woods. I went back and forth, calling and calling. 'Papa! It's Alicia! Papa, where are you?'"

Exhausted and grief-stricken, Alicia faced the truth; her father would not be coming back. He was gone, and so was the life she had known. Years later, writing about her experiences, she chronicled the destruction of her family:

```
First they killed my brother Moshe. . . .
Then they killed my father. . . .
Then they killed my brother Bunio. . . .
Then they killed my brother Zachary. . . .
Then they killed my last brother, Herzl.
```

Running From Death

In the months to come, Alicia would fall into enemy hands three times. The first time, she ended up in a sealed boxcar on the way to a Nazi death camp. She escaped because two men loosened the steel bars from a small window, and began pushing children off the train.

When Alicia jumped out, a bush broke her fall, leaving her bruised and scratched but otherwise intact. She watched as the train with its human cargo crested the grade and disappeared from sight. Then she did the only thing she could think to do: followed the railroad tracks back home.

In December 1942, Alicia was picked up again and sent to a notorious prison near the town of Chortkov, where she was beaten senseless and left for dead. A Jewish burial detail literally snatched her from the grave and took her to a kindly Jewish couple who nursed her back to health.

Alicia returned to Buczacz only to be caught up in the final liquidation of the ghetto. To make the city *Judenrein*, or free of Jews, the Nazis sent some to death camps and others to a ghetto in the town of Kopechince. At first, the Jurman family considered themselves very fortunate to be chosen for the ghetto. Then an *Einsatzgruppe*, or death squad, swept into town.

The Killing Field

Einsatzgruppen units did not fight with the regular army. They would follow the regular army around, and, after the regular army left, they had one job to complete: to slaughter every last Jew in every town they passed. Alicia managed to hide her mother and little brother, but she could not hide herself. Along with other Jews from the ghetto, she was marched to a field outside of town. The first thing she noticed was a freshly-dug trench making an ugly brown scar on the land:

> There were many Jews at the trench already, some undressed and some still undressing. Then the shooting started. We were pushed from the back by the barrels of machine guns and, as we approached the trench, we were confronted by more machine guns. Some people in front fell into the trench dead, and some still alive. . . . [A]s I was nearing the pit, I thought I heard my name being called.[2]

The next thing Alicia heard was machine gun fire, coming from a new direction. Then there was a voice, shouting her name: "Alicia, run! Get out of here! Run!"

Both the voice and the machine gun belonged to a friend from Buczacz. Alicia ran, hard and fast, across the meadow and into the woods beyond. She ran until her legs trembled and her breath came in heavy, painful gasps. Then she collapsed on the ground and cried.

Alicia managed to escape a mass execution after being marched to a field by an Einsatzgruppe. This Ukrainian Jew kneels above a mass grave before being executed by a member of an Einsatzgruppe.

Reunion

Alone in a strange part of the country, Alicia had no idea how to get home. She did know one thing, though: if her mother and brother were still alive, she would find them in Buczacz. In the meantime, she needed food. She made her way to farm country, hoping to find work in the fields.

On her first day, she helped to weed a potato field, for which she received a cup of sour milk and a small piece of bread. The next day she moved on to another farm, then another, and yet another. She worked hard and said as little as possible about her personal life. Alicia finally made her way to Buczacz and found her mother, but not her little brother. He had disappeared from Kopechince, and had not been found. Mother and daughter had to go on alone. They left Buczacz as quickly as possible, taking back roads through farm country. Mrs. Jurman was too weak to work in the fields, and, in any case, could easily be spotted as a Jew. She hid during the day, while Alicia worked at surrounding farms.

Alicia, Helka, and Slavka

Some of the farms where Alicia worked belonged to Poles and others to Ukrainians. Because these two groups did not like one another, Alicia crafted two identities for herself: "Helka" for the Poles, and "Slavka" for the Ukrainians:

```
I had to be careful approaching the farmers
to ask for work; what if I addressed one in
Ukrainian and he turned out to be Polish?
He would certainly turn me away, and then
I would have lost the chance to work and
get a piece of bread for my mother. On
the other hand, if I spoke Polish to a
```

> Ukrainian, something even worse could
> happen—the man might come after me with
> his shovel. So the first moment that I
> approached the farmers was always crucial.
> On my way across the field I always tried
> to swing close to other workers and listen
> to their conversation to find out what
> language to use. If I had no choice and had
> to approach the farmer directly, I mumbled
> my greeting and waited to find out in what
> language he would answer.[3]

Along the way, Alicia made friends with an elderly Pole whose epileptic seizures made him an outcast. Superstitious neighbors thought he was possessed by a demon. In time, his tiny cottage became a safe haven for the Jurmans and other Jewish families. With a safe place for her mother, Alicia could wander as far as necessary to find work.

Germans on the Run

March 24, 1944, was a day Alicia would never forget. Soviet troops liberated the area they were living in, forcing the Germans into full retreat. Alicia and her mother made their way back to Buczacz, not quite knowing what to do. In this way, they were not alone:

> Everyone—and by that I mean about two
> hundred and fifty Jewish survivors—was in
> a daze, filled with a terrible feeling of
> loss and pain. I remember waking up several
> times each night during those first days
> because the bed was actually shaking with
> my mother's silent, convulsive sobbing.
> I knew that she waited until after I was

Adolf Hitler looks at the bomb damage to a German city in 1944. The German army was on the run when Alicia's town was liberated by Soviet troops in March 1944.

asleep to release her grief and longing
for my father and my brothers, and so
I pretended to be asleep each time this
happened.[4]

After two months of freedom, Alicia and her mother, along with the other Jews of Buczacz, were beginning to think about rebuilding their lives. Then the unthinkable happened: the Nazis came back. When their artillery bombarded the city, Mrs. Jurman got hit by a piece of shrapnel and lost a great deal of blood. Alicia managed to get her mother back to their apartment, but there would be no running this time.

"As we stood there shivering, clinging to each other, one of the SS men stepped back, drew his pistol, and aimed it right at me."

Mrs. Jurman had other ideas: "You must go, Alicia. . . . You must survive. You are the only witness to what happened to our family, to our people"[5]

Alicia could not bring herself to leave, and so mother and daughter waited. They hoped for the best, but they were not surprised when SS men kicked in the door and ordered them into the street:

As we stood there shivering, clinging
to each other, one of the SS men stepped
back, drew his pistol, and aimed it right
at me. . . .
What happened next only added to the
nightmare. I heard the gun go off, and
suddenly my mother lay dead at my feet.
She had thrown herself between me and my
murderer and had been hit by the bullet
meant for me.[6]

The SS man pointed his gun at Alicia and pulled the trigger, but nothing happened. He tried again, but still nothing. He was out of ammunition: "I will never know why he did not reload or why the other SS man did not shoot me, but for some reason they decided to take me to prison instead."

Once more, Alicia was marched to a killing field—the very meadow where the SS had killed her father. A fresh trench waited to be filled with bodies. Alicia positioned herself at one end of the line and, at the first opportunity, made a run for the woods.

So the running began again, and Alicia had no idea when it might end. Part of her wanted to give up—sit down somewhere and quit struggling. But she remembered what her mother had said about surviving, so she kept going. It was the only thing she could think to do.

****

Alicia survived the war, but she did not stop moving. At a time when Palestine had immigration quotas, she smuggled Holocaust survivors into eretz Israel. She went to Israel, but she did not stay. She met and married Gabriel Appleman, an American Jew, and went with him to the United States. There, she could finally start building a new life.

Thousands of Jews survived the Holocaust with stories such as Alicia's. Many lived on the run, seeking refuge wherever they could find it. Sometimes, they found people willing to help them. But often, Jews could only rely on themselves to survive.

Chapter Two

THE RIGHT TIME TO GO

Adolf Hitler burst upon the stage of German politics when President Paul von Hindenburg named him chancellor, or head of state, in 1933. Hitler told the German people that they were a "master race," destined to rule the world. He also told them that Jews did not share this destiny. He said the Jews were a corrupt and vicious "race," scheming for world domination.

Step by step, Hitler and his Nazis transformed antisemitic ideas into antisemitic policies and actions in Germany. In April 1933, Hitler called for a one-day boycott of all Jewish shops. In May, crowds of young people burned hundreds of books written by Jews and anti-Nazis.

In 1934, all Jewish students were excluded from exams in medicine, dentistry, pharmacy, and law, and in 1935, one of the provisions of the Nuremberg Laws stripped Jews of their German citizenship.

As German Jews lost their jobs, their property, and their civil rights, thousands decided to run while they still had the chance. They went to other European countries, to the Americas, to Asia— to any place that would take them. By 1938, about one-third of Germany's five hundred thousand Jews had left the country. The two-thirds who stayed clung to the hope that life would somehow get back to normal. This did not happen. Instead, the situation for Jews in Germany went from bad to worse.

Poverty and Desperation

Hundreds, then thousands, of German-Jewish men lost their jobs or businesses. At that time, most women did not work outside the home. They ran the household and cared for the children. The task of earning a living fell to the men. When they could no longer perform this task, whole families plunged into desperate poverty.

Jewish men in these dire straits reacted in different ways. Liane Reif-Lehrer's father sank into depression after he lost his thriving dental practice. He eventually decided that the family would have to leave, regardless of the many hardships this would entail:

> So [my parents] went and applied for visas and passports and so on. On the morning of September 30, 1938, my father and mother actually left the house together to go pick up those passports. They picked up the passports and at about noontime, they parted to do separate chores. . . . I guess at about 2:30 in the afternoon . . . there was a phone call. My father had been found at the bottom of a staircase. I'm not sure whether he was already dead or whether he died either on the way to the hospital or right after he got to the hospital. But the death certificate says that he died of multiple fractures including a fractured skull and lots of fractured ribs. . . . [The] general consensus was that he had committed suicide. My mother didn't want anybody to know that and . . . I never, ever said anything until quite recently about that. . . . My brother's idea is that

A portrait of Liane Reif-Lehrer with her dog taken on
January 15, 1937, in Vienna, Austria. Her family decided
to flee the country, despite the hardships they would face.

> my father probably did commit suicide and
> that one of the reasons that he did it,
> aside from being depressed . . . was that
> he probably figured that a woman with two
> children would have a much better chance of
> escaping if there was no husband around. At
> that time, mostly it was the men who were
> being really harassed.[1]

Kristallnacht and Beyond

The antisemitic violence of November 9–10, 1938, convinced many Jews that it was time to flee Germany. In Jewish neighborhoods, synagogues, homes, and businesses went up in flames. Shattered glass littered the sidewalks. This attack came to be known as *Kristallnacht*, the night of broken glass. According to Nazi propaganda, it was a "spontaneous" demonstration of outrage because a Jewish student had shot and killed a German embassy official in Paris.

Actually, the violence of Kristallnacht was not spontaneous at all. On November 10, 1938, a telegram from the SS (special security force) directed local officials to carry out violence against Jews. It further ordered mass arrests of "healthy male Jews, who are not too old."[2] In response to this order, thirty thousand Jews were arrested and sent to concentration camps.[3]

Fred Ederer's parents were making plans to escape Germany when the Nazis began their roundup:

> My parents . . . discussed a strategy for
> dealing with the Nazis, who, according to
> my parents, were sure to pay us a call . . .
> [and] would be looking for money and other

valuables. My parents mainly expressed concern about the two bank books providing access to the funds we needed to booking passage to the United States. We expected to be able to emigrate in December, when our quota numbers for the American visas were due to come up. . . . My mother sewed into the back of the boys' pajama tops the two bankbooks—one bankbook into each pajama top. My brother and I went to bed early, as my parents hoped that the Nazis would neither disturb the children nor discover the bank books. My mother prepared 30 marks in cash to turn over when they asked for money. My parents stayed up and waited.

They came at 11 o'clock, four of them—two SS-men . . . and two civilians. I was fully awake, but pretended to be asleep. They asked for money and my mother gave them the 30 marks. They then searched all the rooms, including the room my brother and I were in, and took all the jewelry and silverware they could find, which was essentially all of it. They did not disturb us children and did not find the bank books.

Finally before they left, I heard them ask my father to put on his coat—he was to go with them. . . . My father pleaded that he had never done anything wrong and that an Austrian colleague of his who had been a long-standing member of the Nazi party would vouch for him. . . . At long last, the men left—miraculously without my father.

The next day we learned that my father was the only adult male resident of the

The antisemitic violence of Kristallnacht convinced many Jews that it was time to leave Germany. Local residents had to watch this synagogue burn to the ground in Ober-Ramstadt, Germany, on November 10, 1938.

apartment house who had been spared; all
the other men, about 20, had been taken
away—to Dachau [a concentration camp]. . . .
By the time we left . . . for the United
States (January 19, 1939), the men had not
returned. . . .

Kristallnacht was a clear signal to all
the world that there were no limits to Nazi
atrocities and served ample notice to Jews
in Germany that there was no hope other
than emigration—if only a safe haven
could be found. Unfortunately, the few
safe havens that existed were open to only
a relatively small number of Jews.[4]

When Time Ran Out

"Unfortunately, the few safe havens that existed were open to only a relatively small number of Jews."

Considering the danger of living under German control, many have wondered why more Jews did not get out early. Some stayed because they had no place to go, or did not have enough money for the trip. Some tried to get out, only to find that they had run out of time.

Gerda Feldman was a teenager living in Germany when Kristallnacht tore her world apart. Looking back, she talked about why so many had waited too long:

We had a grocery store. Once or twice my
father was beaten up in the dark when he
came home from the shop. And then things
got a little difficult. But you see, when
you're sort of 12, 13, you don't quite
realize the dangers that were going on. . . .
People always say to me, "Why did people

not leave early on?," and the only theory
I can have is, if you are very poor you can
go because you've got nothing to lose, and
if you were rich, you know at the beginning
you were allowed to take your money out
with you, but if you are a middle-class
person then you sort of value a little bit
of security.[5]

Closing Doors

After Kristallnacht, thousands of desperate Jews clamored to get out of Germany, only to find they had nowhere to go. Four months earlier, representatives from thirty-two countries had gathered in Evian, France.

For nine days, they discussed the plight of European Jews without deciding on any kind of unified policy. In the end, only the Dominican Republic agreed to open its borders to Jewish refugees. Other countries, including the United States, Great Britain, France, and Canada, feared that a flood of immigrants with no means of supporting themselves would become a drain on their economies.

While trapped Jews struggled to survive, Europe braced for war. It began on September 1, 1939, when Germany invaded Poland. The Polish army tried to mount a defense, but the German army overwhelmed them with a fierce assault that Hitler called *blitzkrieg* ("lightning war"). Poland fell in just three weeks. Under the terms of a secret pact with the Soviet Union, the Germans did not take all of Poland. They only occupied the western part of the country, up to the River Bug. The Soviets took the territory east of the river.

Evian, France, was the site of the International Conference on Refugees, where thirty-two nations discussed the plight of Europe's Jews. The town of Evian is shown in this 1938 postcard.

Where to Go, What to Do

After the German invasion of Poland, in Nazi-occupied Warsaw, some young Jews wanted to get away from the Germans at all costs. According to fifteen-year-old Simha Rotem, these Jews

```
organized in small groups, planning to go
east, cross the River Bug, and get to the
Russian-occupied zone. One of them was my
```

cousin Simha . . . who was two or three years older than me. I wanted to go with him but my parents wouldn't let me, so I stayed. We got one message and then lost track of him. I don't know what became of him. I urged my parents, especially Father, to let me go to the Soviets, but to no avail. Once I did seem to convince Father, but the issue kept getting postponed. Meanwhile, refugees began returning from the Soviet zone bearing bad news, which didn't encourage moving there.[6]

Yitzhak Zuckerman worked in Warsaw with a Zionist youth group that prepared teenagers and young adults to settle in Palestine (present-day Israel). He never forgot the day that changed his life. When the war began September 1, many cities were bombed, causing serious casualties, and everything was in an uproar. Yitzhak was in the village of Klebán at the time, having gone there for a conference. He raced back to Warsaw to discuss the situation with his colleagues in the movement: "By then we knew from the radio about the German advance. We figured that our Movement would retreat eastward, but it didn't occur to us that Poland wouldn't hold out at all, not even a few months."[7]

Poland was only the beginning. One nation after another was crushed by Hitler's blitzkrieg: Denmark, Norway, Belgium,

Yitzhak Zuckerman delivering a speech at a Zionist meeting sometime shortly after the war. Prior to the war, Zuckerman worked for a Zionist youth group in Warsaw, Poland.

Luxembourg, the Netherlands, and France. With each new Nazi conquest, thousands of Jews fell under Hitler's control.

Thirteen-year-old Shulamit Perlmutter (later, Charlene Schiff) lived in the Ukrainian town of Horochow, near the Polish border. The Germans did not get there until June 1941. As soon as they took control of the place, they set up a ghetto for the Jews. This involved choosing a crumbling old neighborhood and forcing all Jews to live there. Shulamit lived in the ghetto with her mother and sister until 1942, when they heard rumors that the ghetto was about to be destroyed. Her mother began looking for a hiding place:

> [Mother] wanted to find a place where someone would hide the three of us. . . . One day, she came home and she was very excited, and she told us that she found two places. She couldn't find one place where the farmer or the people would be willing to hide three people, so she found two. One place would hide one person, and another place, the people were willing to take two people. And, there was my mother's difficult decision, how and who should go where. And in her infinite wisdom, she decided that my sister, being the older one, would be able to manage on her own, and mother and I would go to the other place, the two of us. . . . The plans were that [the farmer] would pick her up after work one evening, and that one morning when we all got up, we ate our meager breakfast, and my sister took her little bundle with her, the most important things, clothing that she still had. She wasn't crying,

At thirteen, Shulamit never saw her mother again after hiding
from the Nazis in a river. She survived the war hiding in the forest.
Shulamit (now Charlene Schiff) is pictured at left in this photo taken
in a displaced persons camp after the war.

and I wasn't crying either. We hugged, we embraced, and we said goodbye, and my mother kept saying how wonderful it would be when all this is over, we'll meet again, and papa will come home and we'll have great celebrations. And so, she and my sister went to work, and that evening my mother came back by herself, and she told me that my sister went off and everything was working according to her plan. . . .

A few days after my sister left, my mother came home from work and she says, "It's time to go." And so, she made me dress in my best clothes, and again, I still had that coat with a few sewn-in coins, and I put on my high-top shoes, and she got dressed . . . and made two little bundles, one for myself and one for her. We ate our meager supper, and when it got dark, really dark, . . . [we] walked out, we didn't say goodbye to anyone. And pretty soon we were in the river. . . . All of a sudden shots rang out, and we ducked . . . we just stayed there . . . the entire night. . . . The next morning, [we] . . . heard a lot of noise, a lot of commotion, we saw fire, we heard screams, we heard babies crying. . . . A lot of other people from the ghetto tried to do the very same thing we did, and they ran towards the river. . . . At that time, the guards started screaming, the Ukrainian guards. . . . "Crawl out, Jew, I can see you.". . . My mother held me down and we stayed put. . . . I don't know how many days we stayed in the river, but it was several days, and I kept

> dozing off. And one time I woke up, or I
> thought I woke up, and I looked around, and
> my mother wasn't there.[8]

Shulamit Perlmutter never saw her mother again. At the age of thirteen, Shulamit had become an orphan. She managed to survive by hiding in the forest near Horochow, scavenging for food and keeping far away from other people.

The world became a place of horror for orphans like Shulamit. Some tried to run, some went into hiding, and some were too paralyzed by fear to do anything. All had one thing in common: the Holocaust had forced them out of a normal life and into a world gone mad.

Chapter Three

THE SEARCH FOR REFUGE

The search for refuge in countries under German control was both complicated and dangerous. Some used false identification papers, hoping they would not be caught. Others tried to find a country that would give them visas. Still, others slipped across international borders without papers. Regardless of what they did or where they went, young people quickly learned that uncertainty and fear were an inescapable part of their lives. They also learned that success or failure could turn on the most trivial of incidents.

Two Families

In March 1939, teenager Ursula Bacon and her parents were waiting for a train that would take them out of Germany. Ursula noticed another family:

> A quietly dressed, middle-aged couple with two girls about twelve and fourteen years of age were standing amidst their four pieces of luggage at the edge of the crowd just outside the terminal. A couple of Hitler's brown-shirted SA men swaggered by, stopped at the little family which was most probably fleeing the country just as we were. The four people seemed to be shrinking into each other in a futile attempt to become invisible. One of the SA men made

some remark that caused them both to break out in coarse, boisterous laughter. The other Nazi began twirling an iron crowbar expertly in the air, and with calculated accuracy suddenly brought it down hard on one of the family's . . . suitcases. The sharp points of the iron tool ripped a deep gash into the leather. In order to retrieve his weapon from the suitcase, the man yanked sharply, the rip widened, and with a death-knoll tinkling, several gold coins escaped from their hiding place between the leather and the lining. The gold pieces twinkled and danced on the marble floor for a brief moment, then came to rest at the . . . feet of the two Nazis.

"The mother, the father, and the two . . . girls would most probably not live to leave Germany."

My father stood still as a rock, his eyes averted, glued to the floor. He was gritting his teeth so hard that I could hear a crunching sound. A strong muscle jumped on his right cheek, ready to burst through and attack the world. Mother's hand flew to her mouth as she stifled a soundless scream. Within seconds, shouting an endless barrage of Jew-swine-filthy-Jew curses and insults, the two burly Brownshirts herded the family on a fast trot out into the street and out of our sight, pulling the treacherous luggage behind them on a small cart. The mother, the father, and the two . . . girls would most probably not live to leave Germany.[1]

Ursula's family was luckier. The train took them to Genoa, Italy, where they made connections with a steamship bound for sanctuary in Shanghai, China. "WE MADE IT! We escaped!" Ursula wrote:

> Father, Mother, and I made it out of Germany in the middle of a cold, fog-shrouded March night. Stealing out of town like thieves, leaving the scene of the crime of being Jewish. I shall never, ever forget those last few days we spent at home. Horror, fear, and panic closed in on us like an evil fog, sinister and unforgiving. Like the whirlpools of a gray and churning river it threatened to pull us down, swallow us, and leave no sign of us behind. I don't want to remember getting my father out of the Gestapo prison. I'm petrified that just thinking about it could bring it all back. But we made it; we did!
>
> At last, we were on board our ship. There I was—tucked away in my little pocket of a cabin adjacent to the bigger one of my parents, about to sail on the steamship *Gneisenau*, on our way to China.[2]

Even in her joy, Ursula could not stop thinking about the family at the train station.

Special Targets

When the Nazis took over a town, they imprisoned or killed local government officials and any prominent Jews. They believed that taking away the leaders made the rest of the population easier to control. Leo Melamed's father faced special danger because he

This is the Certificate of Polish Nationality that Leo Melamed and his mother used to leave Vilna, Lithuania, for Japan. It was issued December 5, 1939.

was both a Jew and a city councilman in Bialystok, Poland. When the Germans invaded, Mr. Melamed went into hiding with the rest of the council.

Leo kept a clear memory of that time:

> My mother woke me in the middle of the night to tell me that I must get dressed; she's taking me to say goodbye to my father. The city was being bombed, and you could hear the air raid sirens and the "Aak aak" of anti-aircraft guns echoing through the buildings as we ran. My father embraced me, not knowing of course whether and when he was coming back and I of course knew nothing. And to leave us behind, not knowing what would happen, was the most difficult decision of his life.
>
> [Later] my father called, and said that it was imperative for my mother and me to take the train out of Bialystok to Wilno [Vilna], that very night. My mother hurriedly packed a small suitcase with just enough for a few days, because that's all she thought we were going for. The train station [was] a madhouse. It was the last train out of Bialystok, and the whole family—my grandmothers and my aunt—came to the [train station] to say goodbye. But everyone knew it was just a temporary thing. This was until things straightened out and we would be right back. We never came back.[3]

Leo's father eventually caught up to his wife and son, and the reunited family began a long journey that would take them through the frozen wastelands of Siberia to a temporary safe haven in Japan. In 1941, the Melameds settled in the United States and made it their home.

Looking back on those years, Leo remembered the constant uncertainty:

> You got used to the transitory life that you were leading and that there was no certainty. And you got used to that and it's part of being a refugee. It's a mentality that sets in. Everything is temporary. You don't know where you're going, where you're going to be. You may be here for a long time, you may be here for a short time. . . . [We] had no knowledge of the fact that we would be given permission to the United States or anywhere else. We didn't know if we were going to stay in . . . Japan forever. We didn't know where else we would go. . . . [That's] the life of a refugee. The unknown becomes part of your keeping, part of your life.[4]

Leo Melamed lived in Japan until immigrating to the United States in 1941. Melamed received this wooden crayon case while studying at a Japanese school.

The family that remained in Poland did not survive: "[B]oth my grandmothers and my aunt—together with some 500 other Jews were crammed into . . . the [Bialystok synagogue]. The entire building was gasolined and torched, and they all died."[5]

Into the Unknown

Like the Melameds, many Jews had to leave family members behind. Some agonized over the decision, while others barely had time to think about it. Their lives depended on quick thinking and even quicker action. Eva Rappoport was not yet a teenager when her family made a hasty escape from the Nazis:

> My parents decided we had to leave Vienna [Austria] and that our only chance was to go to France and it was really a last-minute decision and very hurriedly we decided to leave everything behind. . . . And I remember . . . my mother telling me that I was to go to my room and just pick the few toys that I wanted to take with me and be fast about it. . . . [I] started piling up . . . my things and my favorite dolls and mother . . . said, "Oh, no. You can't take all this," and she picked two dolls, and she said, "You can take two dolls. Period." And I was crying . . . [because] I thought it was terribly unfair to do this to me. . . . And so we . . . just threw some clothes in suitcases and . . . we went and said goodbye to my grandparents. . . . That was the last time that I . . . was [ever] to see them again.[6]

The Risk of Waiting

Even people who decided to flee did not always realize the importance of getting out promptly. Edith Schleissner lived with her parents in Prague, Czechoslovakia. The first she had heard of Hitler was in March 1938, when Germany took over Austria: "When Austria fell . . . Mama, who had read Mein Kampf [Hitler's book] and believed every word, begged my father to flee to Paris, but he scoffed at her fears."[7]

In September 1938, Great Britain pressured Czechoslovakia to cede (give up) its Sudetenland region to Germany. Hitler assured Czechoslovakia and Britain that he was satisfied to have this strip of land on the German border.

Many Czechoslovakian Jews did not believe Hitler's assurances. The government started preparing for war and Jews started leaving Prague. Edith's father finally saw the danger and made plans to leave. He bought train tickets for March 10th:

> Unexpectedly, [my grandfather] died on March 8, and his funeral was the next day. Mama wanted to leave as scheduled, but Papa insisted that the least he could do to show respect for his father was to sit Shiva [a Jewish mourning ritual] for the required eight days. It was an argument with which Mama could not disagree.[8]

The decision to stay turned out to be very badly timed. On March 15, 1939, German troops occupied Czechoslovakia. Edith remembered the dreary weather, and the radio announcer telling all children to go to school as usual:

Many Jews did not realize the importance of fleeing the German-occupied territories right away. In Vienna, Austria, civilians welcome the German troops on March 14, 1938.

My parents, who had been so afraid of the event for as long as I could remember, acted as if nothing was different and hurried us out so that we wouldn't be late. But a lot was different. There were olive drab trucks parked all along the curb in front of my school. . . .

Heavily armed soldiers stood at attention at either side of the entrance to the school, just like a pair of book-ends. A similar pair of book-ends stood inside the doorway. In the classroom pictures of Hitler glared at us from the top of each wall. What kind of army, I wondered, bothers lugging along so many pictures for school rooms, when, surely, they had more important things to do? I was also enraged that the Nazis felt they needed guns to protect themselves from little children. The morning was unusually subdued, and by the time we left to go home for lunch, my anger was all consuming. Without thinking of it, I stomped the foot of one of the book-ends and glared into his eyes. Much to my fury, he smiled at me benevolently and ruffled my hair.

"She explained to me that what I had done was very dangerous and could have gotten me shot . . . "

As I stepped out the door, Mama grabbed my arm and dragged me around the corner, away from the school. Then she squatted down to be at eye level with me. Shaking with obvious fear, she explained to me that what I had done was very dangerous and could have gotten me shot; that then I'd be dead and that she and the whole family couldn't bear that. She begged me, with tears in her eyes, to be good and to use self-control, to please, please stop asking questions and try to understand everything. Mama explained that there were things happening that were beyond anyone's understanding. The fact that she didn't get angry with me and that she was pleading with me, made a deep impression. I promised her, and myself, I would do my best to comply.[9]

The city turned nightmarish, and the family knew it was time to leave:

Finally, early on the morning of April 9, we escaped from Prague. Papa had obtained permits allowing the whole family, Babi and Dzeida included, to go to the Tatra mountains [on the Polish-Czechoslovakian border] for Mama's recuperation [from pneumonia]. We were allowed to enter the railroad station, where we made our way to the Paris track. Papa timed it so that when we arrived, he had only enough time to waive the permits under the German guard's nose before the train started to move. We barely caught the last car of the train. We crossed Germany uneventfully. At the border to France, ours was the last com-partment to be examined by both countries' border guards. Once again Papa waived the . . . permits under the German noses, and the French made them run off the train, as by then it was moving into France.[10]

The Schleissners arrived safely in Paris, but they would not be safe there for long because Germany invaded France in 1940. In their flight from the Nazis, they went to the Normandy Coast of France, Spain, Portugal, and finally the United States.

Another Last Goodbye

For some, the decision to separate was more deliberate. Evelyn Konrad's father got visas for himself, his wife, and Evelyn, but not for Evelyn's grandmother. Other relatives tried to get her a visa, but without success.

In time, the family had to face a hard truth; there was nothing to do but leave Evelyn's grandmother behind. Evelyn never forgot the day she and her mother went to say goodbye:

> We walked up the stone stairs to my [grandmother's] apartment. A skinny woman with feverish eyes, dressed all in black, opened up the door, face pale and drawn. She pointed to the front hallway and to my [grandmother's] bedroom, which was at the top of the long hallway. My mother thanked her, and the woman shrugged and walked back into another room, closing the door behind her. There were muffled sounds behind all the doors as we passed on the way to my [grandmother].
>
> "Who's there?" I heard her say behind her closed door in a strangled whisper, even though she knew that my mother and I were due that day.
>
> "Mutti," my mother said. The bedroom door was flung open, and my [grandmother] pulled us in, first me, and then my mother.

Edith Schleissner and her family escaped Prague in the nick of time. Her father had obtained papers to get them to France. Her family's journey continued to Spain, Portugal, and the United States. This is a French travel visa that was used to go to the United States.

```
Then she closed the door again and turned
the key in the door.
     She looked less stout than she had been.
Smothering me to her breast, she hugged me
and kissed me and said, "Greterl, take the
child out of here. Go back and take the
first train. Please."11
```

Evelyn and her mother took the train to France, "but on the whole journey my mother sat in a corner crying, quietly, without a sound, and without stopping. I had never known that anyone could find tears for so many hours."[12] Evelyn's grandmother died on a transport to Treblinka, a Nazi death camp.

An Instinct for Survival

Many refugees had to make life-or-death decisions with little or no information. In the absence of facts, some people could not choose at all; they could only await whatever might happen to them. Others relied on "instincts" or "hunches" to decide their course of action.

When the Germans invaded Lithuania in June 1941, Roza Weintraub's instincts led her to strike out on her own. She was in Vilna when the Nazis began bombarding the country: "We heard aeroplanes, we heard sirens, but we thought they were drills. . . . [Father] said: 'No, it is War,' and I should stay in Vilna, that I must not leave the place."[13]

Sometime later, Roza's father changed his mind:

```
He goes home and he thinks that the safest
place for us would be in Kibart, in our
town, where our friends were, until the end
of the war, as long as it takes. There is
```

```
no place like home. . . . At this time I
was staying with a woman. We had spent the
night in the basement. We decided to run
away. If you'd asked me why I decided to
run, I don't know. It was some sort of
instinct. . . . I cannot explain.¹⁴
```

Taking a Gamble on Life

In Volozhin, Poland, a Zionist youth group known as "Betar" was already operating when the Germans came. Zionists wanted to build a Jewish homeland in Palestine. Before the war started, going to Palestine was a "some-day" dream. During the war, many young Jews considered it a matter of life and death.

In 1940, sixteen-year-old Chaya Szepsenwol [now Lucille] and her older sister Feiga were members of Betar. Chaya remembered the night her sister came

> "If you'd asked me why I decided to run, I don't know. It was some sort of instinct. . . . I cannot explain."

back from a Betar meeting with important news: "[The members] decided they were going to try to get to Vilna, and they thought well maybe from Vilna they would try to get to Israel. . . . [M]y mother thought [Feiga] was out of her mind. . . . But [Feiga] was . . . insistent and my mother realized that things were getting pretty rough."¹⁵

Once Chaya's mother had made up her mind, she did not look back. She helped pack two small suitcases and took the girls to the train station: "There were thousands, thousands of people trying to get on the train. My mother just pushed us on the train, and . . .

Chaya (right) and Feiga Szepsenwol left Poland for Vilna, Lithuania. This portrait was taken of the sisters in Kovno, Lithuania, the day they received their exit visas to Japan.

sort of threw [our suitcases] after us [as] the train took off. We never got even a chance to say good-bye to her."[16]

The girls made it to Vilna, but nothing had come of the Betar's idea about going to Palestine. The two sisters were alone in a strange city, with no place to go. They managed to rent a furnished room while they considered the problem.

The solution to their problem came in the form of a rumor. A diplomat at the Japanese embassy in Kovno was handing out hundreds of exit visas for Japan. The girls decided to go to his office in Kovno to see if they could get one. They did not know that they were about to meet one of the heroes of the Holocaust, Chiune Sugihara. For twenty-nine days in July and August of 1940, he and his wife Yukiko wrote more than three hundred visas per day. Those visas that Sugihara gave out allowed thousands of Jews to find refuge in Japan.

In Kovno, long lines of desperate people circled the Japanese embassy. Chaya remembered standing in one of those lines:

```
It was like about three or four o'clock
in the afternoon and the office was closing
at 5:00 or 5:30, and we saw that it was
getting too close, that we would probably
not be able to get in, so at one point
where the door opened, I grabbed my
sister's hand and we just ran up the stairs
and we tried to get in. And of course we
tried to cross the line, so they pushed us
down and we were right back on the bottom
of the steps. We felt we were not going to
make it that day. Finally we took courage
again and we ran up those stairs, and I
just put my foot right in the door, as they
```

Chiune Sugihara sitting at his desk in Kovno, Lithuania. As Japanese consul in Lithuania, he issued thousands of visas that allowed fleeing Jews refuge in Japan. Chaya and Feiga each received a visa from Sugihara.

say, and was holding on to my sister, and
we got in. We saw Mr. Sugihara. He asked
us our name, he asked us where our parents
were. We told him, my father was not living,
my mother had no papers, and he looked very
sympathetic at us and he just stamped, gave
us the visa right there, on the spot. My
sister and I got hysterical, we were just
so happy, and there was a photographer
walking around and he asked if we want to
take our picture, so I have two pictures
of my sister and myself on that day.
August 12, 1940.[17]

Like other young refugees, Chaya and Feiga grew up quickly
while they were on the run. They became clever and quick-witted,
bold when they needed to be. Under ordinary circumstances, well-
mannered Jewish teenagers did not barge into foreign embassies.
However, circumstances during the Holocaust were very far from
ordinary.

Chapter Four

TWO JOURNEYS

Two rescue operations have earned a special place in Holocaust history: the *Kindertransport* program and the voyage of the ocean liner *St. Louis*. Both occurred in the shadow of Kristallnacht, when Jews saw their synagogues torched, their homes and businesses vandalized, and more than thirty thousand Jewish men imprisoned in Dachau and other Nazi concentration camps.[1] Most of these men were later released, on the condition that they get out of Germany as soon as possible.

For many Jewish families "as soon as possible" was never. The Nazis had thrown them out of their jobs, taken their valuables, and frozen their bank accounts. Jews who managed to scrape together enough money to leave could not find a place to go. Other nations would not open their doors to such large numbers of refugees.

The Kindertransport Begins

In Britain, relief organizations set out to save those who could be saved: the children.

They set to work immediately after Kristallnacht, screening applicants, arranging transportation, and finding places for the children to live. An appeal for donations to pay for this expensive program quickly produced 550,000 pounds (over a million U.S. dollars)—a fortune in 1939.

The program accepted children between the ages of six months to sixteen years. To pay for the individual living expenses, each child had to guarantee a bond of fifty pounds (about 1,500.00 dollars). Whenever possible, families posted this bond, but private donors came forward to help those who could not afford it.

The first transport left Germany by train on December 1, 1938, and arrived in England the next day, with two hundred children from a Jewish orphanage in Berlin. This first transport established a pattern that many others would follow. Children from small towns were taken to collection points in major cities, such as Berlin (Germany), Vienna (Austria), and Prague (Czechoslovakia). From there, they traveled by train to seaports in the Netherlands or Belgium, then by boat to the coast of England.

Children stand on deck aboard the first Kindertransport arriving in Harwich, England, on December 2, 1938. Two hundred children from an orphanage in Germany went to England during this trip.

In England, volunteers sent each child to his or her temporary home. Some lived in private homes as members of the family. Others went to hostels, boarding schools, children's homes, or other facilities that could accommodate sizeable groups. Some teenagers were assigned to jobs as farm hands or household help. Neither the parents nor the children had any control over where and with whom the children would live.

Saying Goodbye

With so little information, parents who put their children into the Kindertransport program had to deal with uncertainty, grief, and some well-meaning people who second-guessed their decision. Alice Ebostarkova (Masters) was fourteen when her parents sent her and her two sisters to England:

> [T]he fact that my parents agreed to send us will be a mystery for as long as I live. . . . [E]verybody said to them, "How can you do that? How can you send your children away? Nothing is going to happen here." But my parents started to work very hard towards getting us out. That [meant] that my father had to spend an awful lot of money to get . . . the passports for the three of us. Then my mother started to sew and to accumulate clothes for three years ahead, all sized up to the ages of each of us for three years. . . . My father got the passports. My mother packed. We all had our

"The morning that we were leaving we heard . . . my father cry for the first time. I've never heard my father cry."

suitcases. And one day they said, "You're going to visit [your uncle] in London." . . . Then my older sister was the one who was made to take care of us. . . . She was instructed very carefully . . . that she would be the acting mother; she was 15. . . . Had she been one month older, she wouldn't have been able to get on the transport because the transport only took . . . children from six months to 16 [years].[2]

Alice's parents tried to be matter-of-fact about the parting, but they did not entirely fool their daughters:

The morning that we were leaving we heard . . . my father cry for the first time. I've never heard my father cry. . . . We were all packed to go, and suddenly we heard this noise coming from another room. And we looked at each other in horror because my father was weeping. . . . That's when we realized how awful it's going to be.

[When] we got to the [railroad] station . . . there were hundreds of people, parents and children, little babies. And we were put on a train. My mother couldn't decide whether to keep . . . my younger sister [age 10], so she put her on the train; she took her off. She put her on the train; she took her off again. And then she put her on the train at the last moment. . . . Everyone was crying. The kids were crying. The parents were crying. The train pulled away, and we all waved goodbye and that was it.[3]

A Social Worker Remembers

Norbert Wollheim saw hundreds of these goodbyes. He was one of the organizers of the Kindertransport program and later became coordinator for the transports. It was his job to keep the system moving: watching the timetables, speaking to groups of anxious parents, matching living children with names on a list.

In the course of these duties Wollheim saw hundreds of sad goodbyes:

[I]t was my function to see to it that these things were working properly. . . . [O]n a typical day we asked the parents to come with the children. . . . And there was a very special atmosphere in the air, expectation to a certain extent, there was laughing, and there were tears, and there was concern, and the last . . . advice by the mothers [about] what to do and what not to do, and . . . [when] the time of departure . . . came closer, and we had . . . reserved wagons which . . . had to be filled with these children. And . . . the police had insisted that the parents do not accompany the . . . children to the railways because there were certain difficulties. . . . They insisted that the goodbye had to be done . . . not in . . . public. So . . . when the time of departures came closer . . . I addressed the parents, and told them that the day of departure had come, and they should say goodbye because we're under strict order by the police . . . just to take the children up to the railways and they [the

This identification card issued by the German police revoked the citizenship of a young girl named Inge Engelhard. This card was used in lieu of a passport when she entered England on a Kindertransport and was stamped by immigration authorities.

parents] have to remain there. And . . .
I [asked] for their cooperation and their
understanding, because only that . . .
would guarantee the continuity of our
operations . . . then the parents said
goodbye and again there was laughing and
crying and a last hug. . . . Later [I often
asked] myself the question, "How did I have
the courage to say that to the parents?"
I only can answer that at this time we
didn't know and we couldn't even foresee,
we couldn't surmise for a moment that for
many or most, it would be the last goodbye,
that most of those children would never see
their parents again.[4]

Running Out of Time

Fifteen-year-old Paul Cohn was not aware of these grim facts
when he had to leave his home in Hamburg, Germany, to join the
Kindertransport:

A refugee committee in England had found me
a job on a chicken farm. . . . I was very
sad having to leave my parents behind,
but I was aware that our collective chance
of emigration could improve when I first
traveled to England. My parents appeared to
be in good spirits at our parting, although
they must have had the premonition that we
would not see one another again.

The 4½ hectar chicken farm, with around
5,000 chickens, was owned by a couple who
needed assistance with the work. The actual
work was easy, principally feeding and
watering the birds, and mucking out, but

it involved around 70 hours work a week.
I only had three afternoons free every two
weeks. I had grown up a towny, but I knew
this was the chance of a new life.

I corresponded regularly with my parents
throughout the summer of 1939; I pursued
the possibility
of work for my
parents, e.g. as
housekeeper and
gardener (my father
was an enthusiastic
. . . gardener).
My efforts were
unsuccessful, and
when war broke out
all possibility of emigration ended.

> "I only had three afternoons free every two weeks. I had grown up a towny, but I knew this was the chance of a new life."

From this point on, I only received a
short letter once a month from my parents,
through the Red Cross, that I answered. It
was also sometimes possible to send longer
letters via relatives in America. The letters
became less and less frequent, and at the
end of 1941 they stopped altogether. At the
end of the war I learnt that my parents had
been deported, on 6th December 1941, to
Riga, in Latvia, and had not returned.[5]

Journey From Czechoslovakia

Alice Ebostarkova and her sisters started their journey from
Bratislava, Czechoslovakia, on a route that would take them
through Germany:

[We] were very frightened when we came to
Germany, because . . . there was an inspection.

The German uniformed soldiers came on
the train . . . [and] they inspected our
luggage. And we were frightened, and, of
course, once we left Germany, we were all
thrilled and cheered like crazy. . . .
We were thrilled to be out of Germany and
said, "Now we are—okay, we are safe."

And then we got on the boat.

When we boarded the boat, it was dark—it
was night. And . . . people were sick, and
they were given tea which was the worst
thing I ever tasted in my life. It was
English tea with milk in it. . . . [T]here
were matrons on the boat. . . . I don't
know who they were. Nurses. And we arrived.
I don't remember much about the boat. . . .
I think we tried to sleep. I wish I could
remember more about it.

The boat made port in Harwich, then a train took the children
to Victoria Station in London. The Ebostarkova sisters were in the
midst of what Alice called "an enormous commotion":

[W]e waited and waited for a long time, and
finally our name was called, and there was
our uncle picking us up. And he came with
my guardian, because . . . he had to get a
guardian for each of us. . . . My guardian
was Ms. Fannie Bandit. . . . And she came
. . . to meet us at the station, and my
uncle said, "Now, we are going to drive
to where you are going to live, in Burgess
Hill. It's a children's home." And we
were absolutely shocked about that because
we thought we were going to stay with my
uncle. I didn't know we were going to a

children's home. And . . . I'm not sure, I don't know, well, of course, my uncle, it was weird. I understood why it happened, but my older sister was very upset with my uncle because she thought that he should take my little sister, who was 10 years old. But my uncle was in a very precarious position because he was just newly married, and he had a baby, and they had a small flat in London. And I think his wife was not inclined to take a child, although she says—and she was, she's very close to us

Three Jewish refugee children from Vienna, Austria, pose with their foster family in England after arriving on a Kindertransport. Many children, like Alice Ebostarkova and her sisters, lived with a foster family or in children's homes.

now—I mean, we are very close. She says that, um, she participated, that she was the one who did most of the work to get us . . . out of Czechoslovakia. But she was not the sort of person who wanted to take a child in. I mean, she just, I don't know how that, how that happened. But in any case, the three of us went to this home in Sussex. It was called Wyberley. . . . It was in beautiful grounds, a lovely place, lovely home. And they built sort of an addition to the back of this huge home where . . . the children were being housed. When we arrived, I, well, I can tell you now it was very painful that my uncle took us there.[6]

"When we arrived . . . I can tell you now it was very painful that my uncle took us there."

Alice and her sisters took comfort in letters from their parents, and sometimes packages of items their mother knitted, or fresh homemade cookies; things that were special because they came from home. The letters stopped abruptly in March 1942. Alice knew what that could mean. She was so frightened for her parents that she barely noticed the end of the war. Others could recall exactly where they were and what they were doing when they got the news. Alice could not:

I tried very hard to reconstruct that memory, but . . . I can't. . . . I just don't remember exactly how I found out or where I was. . . . But, of course, we immediately sent cables to Czechoslovakia

> to ask about our parents. And we had
> responses, lots of responses . . . because
> we sent cables to different people asking
> them to find . . . our parents.[7]

The answers to those cables confirmed Alice's worst fears. In June 1942, the Ebostarkovas were sent to Auschwitz and never heard from again.

Far Away From Home

Like Alice Ebostarkova and many others, Inge Sachs had "holes" in her memory. She remembered parts of the long journey from Germany to England, but she did not have clear memories of leaving home:

> [B]eforehand I don't remember what I
> really thought about it. I thought it
> was a necessity. I was homesick, even then,
> before I left home. . . . Everybody was
> preparing to go, so it was nothing special
> that was just for me . . . I don't remember
> the night before [leaving]. My father
> took me to the railway station. I always
> understood that my mother didn't have the
> courage or the strength to take me, but
> I've read recently that only one . . . of
> the parents could take you to the railway
> station. . . . And we were sitting in
> the train, and I remember it was quite a
> cheerful occasion, actually. It was a sort
> of adventure. It wasn't cheerful at all for
> my parents. And then we left. . . . They
> made us sing. And then we came to Hamburg,
> to the port. And there was [passport]
> control, and there were some women who . . .

made a personal search. . . . And then we came on board ship. . . .

I went to Southampton, but there was a stopover in France, in Avri, and we could go make a land excursion, and that was an adventure. . . . I've never been outside Germany . . . and then the boat went on and landed in Southampton and from [there] we went by train. And in Southampton there was a number of ladies who gave each child a box with sweets and sandwich, and so on. And then we went to London, to Waterloo Station. . . . And we sat on wooden benches, and the name was called . . . some youngsters went . . . to a boarding school. Some went to a Quaker organization, and many went to private people who wanted to take a Jewish child in. And I was one of those. [Then] my name was called and the name of the lady who was expecting me. . . . So Mrs. Stevenson [my guardian] took hold of me, and . . . she drove me to her home. . . . She was an elegant woman. I was lucky, she could speak some German.[8]

Inge had trouble adapting to her foster home. Though she never lacked for necessities, the foster home did not show warmth or friendly concerns:

I can tell you one thing that might illustrate [their] coldness. . . . Everybody was going to leave the house, but the house couldn't be left alone. So it was decided that I should stay. So I stayed all [alone] over Christmas in the house. Snow was falling, to make it a picture. Well, when

I learned that I couldn't leave, I couldn't go to my sister, to my relatives, I had the first nervous breakdown crying spell in my life. I couldn't stop myself. Afterwards when it came to the 21st–24th of December, I'd calmed down, but it was very, very hard.[9]

Like Inge Sachs, many of the Kindertransport children lived as strangers in a strange land; never comfortable in their temporary homes, never sure where they stood. They lived with secret grief and with memories they could never erase—but at least they lived. From its beginning in December 1938 to its end in September 1939, the Kindertransport program rescued ten thousand Jewish children from Germany and German-occupied countries.

"Well, when I learned that I couldn't leave, I couldn't go . . . to my relatives, I had the first nervous . . . crying spell in my life."

Out to Sea: Voyage of the *St. Louis*

In April 1939, when Jews were frantic to get out of Germany, the Hamburg-America shipping line announced that its luxury liner, *St. Louis*, would be making a special voyage to Havana, Cuba. Tickets quickly sold out. Of the 937 passengers, almost all of them were Jews fleeing the Nazi Reich. Most of the Jews had bought landing certificates and transit visas from Manuel Benitez, the director of the Cuban immigration office. The *St. Louis* left port from Hamburg, Germany, on May 13, 1939.

For Gerda Feldman, the voyage would become a pleasant escape from the horrors of war. She was fifteen years old when she

Children on the deck of the *St. Louis*. Many youngsters enjoyed the trip to Cuba aboard the luxury cruise liner. Once they arrived, however, the mood changed considerably.

left with her mother and brother aboard the *St. Louis*. Her father was in Poland at the time:

> [My] mother . . . got four passages on the
> . . . St. Louis. . . . The Germans allowed
> people to come back into Germany providing
> they were leaving again. . . . My father
> applied to come back [but] the Poles sent
> [his] brother back [instead], so my father
> didn't make it. And so my father phoned up
> in tears and he told my mother not to go
> without him, and she must have been a very
> determined woman because she said, "I have
> to take the children out." In any case,
> there was another boat leaving after ours
> . . . she couldn't get four passages on
> [that] boat, but one she could get, so
> she was determined to take up three of the
> passages and my father was going to join
> us afterwards on the next boat. . . . The
> finalizations of the visas didn't happen
> until the last minute. We were to leave
> on a Saturday and Friday morning we
> still hadn't [heard] that everything was
> finalized, so my mother rushed off to sort
> things [out] . . . and on Friday afternoon
> . . . she did all the packing and we
> left . . . [on] Friday night.
>
> [F]or us youngsters [the trip] was really
> quite an adventure because this was a luxury
> liner. . . . And it was an experience to
> be on a liner where you had a cinema and
> a ballroom and a swimming pool, and all
> the usual games you have on a boat. . . .
> [So] during the first ten days we really
> had a very good time until we landed.[10]

Awaiting a Verdict

The *St. Louis* arrived at the Havana harbor on May 27. Gerda Blachmann (Wilchfort) was sixteen at the time, traveling with her parents: "We [came] to Havana. But we didn't really dock. We were out . . . far enough so we couldn't even see much of Havana. We just saw the silhouette of the buildings and of the harbor . . . and they told us to come to the dining room with the passports and the visas . . . to be admitted."[11] The Cuban official who came aboard admitted twenty-nine passengers with valid documents, and told the rest to wait until tomorrow.

According to Gerda Feldman, "We . . . were even told to get up very early the next morning and [we] had our breakfast and we lined up with all our suitcases ready to get off, and the boat stopped quite a way outside the harbor. Well, once again we thought that was quite normal, you know, it is [not] always deep enough for the boat to go right into the harbor."[12]

One tomorrow turned into another and then another, and still the passengers could not get straight answers to their questions. While they waited, American President Franklin D. Roosevelt tried to convince the Cuban government to admit the refugees. He could not bring them into the United States without violating the quota system of American immigration law. With Congress and the American people solidly against any such action, Roosevelt could not get the support he needed to accept the *St. Louis* refugees into the United States.

A Final Effort

After a time, the passengers had to admit that their cause was hopeless. Gerda Blachmann remembered:

Refugees aboard the *St. Louis* try to communicate with friends and relatives in Cuba, who could approach the ship in small boats. After reaching the harbor of Havana, Cuba, the passengers were forced to stay on board the ship. Only twenty-nine people got off in Cuba.

[A] terrible mood . . . everybody was very depressed. Few people . . . tried to commit suicide. . . . But you know, humans are always hopeful. . . . [We] always cling to the hope something is going to happen. They're not going to let us rot on the ocean. I mean, something had to happen to us. Of course, the fear was that we would go back to Germany.

[F]irst we came to the coast of Miami. . . . I heard later that the captain had agreed that we make some kind of a forced landing or something but we didn't know anything about it. We just saw the . . . [United States] Coast Guard boats surround us near Miami to make sure that we wouldn't even come close . . . to shore, so that was out. So we saw the lights of Miami. We saw the lights of America and that was it. So we slowly sailed back to Europe.[13]

The Return

Nobody knew what would happen when they got back to Europe. Gerda Feldman called it a "grim atmosphere," and noted that

several . . . people tried to commit suicide and we had a group of young people checking all the cabins to watch people . . . [then] we heard that Belgium, Holland, France, and England were prepared to take a quarter each of the people. . . . [A] lot of people wanted to go England, because the other countries were too near Germany. . . . My father obviously knew what was going on because he sent us a telegram and said:

This is part of the passenger list of the *St. Louis*. Almost all of the Jewish refugees who left Germany aboard the ship returned to Europe.

"Choose England." But really one didn't
have a choice. They decided where
people should go and people's different
nationalities. . . . My mother told
me to go and speak to the . . . English
Immigration Officer because I had learned
English at school. How good my English was
I really don't know, but I did talk to the
man and whether that had any influence or
not I really don't know. But luckily we
ended up in England.[14]

Ending up in England was very lucky indeed. Just a year after the *St. Louis* returned to Europe, Germany conquered Belgium, Holland, and France, but not England. In England, one *St. Louis* refugee died in an air raid. In the occupied nations, a total of 254 *St. Louis* refugees perished along with other Jewish victims.

Both the *St. Louis* passengers and the Kindertransport families took enormous risks to protect themselves and their families. They did what they had to do in spite of their fears and the odds against survival. With this courage, even those who did not survive defied their killers by taking back some control over their lives.

Chapter Five

ONE STEP AHEAD OF DISASTER

Leaving German-controlled countries was only the beginning of escape. Whether traveling with legitimate visas, false papers, or no papers at all, refugees faced danger as long as they were on the move. They could be stopped, searched, and arrested at any time. In crossing national borders, they could be delayed by customs agents or immigration officials.

The Nazi blitzkrieg moved so quickly that many Jews had to live on the run, just to keep ahead of it. In the spring of 1940, German troops overran Denmark, Norway, France, Luxembourg, Holland, and Belgium.

Drastic Measures

When the Nazis invaded Belgium, Alfred Feldman and his family fled into southern France, making their way to the small town of Montagnac:

> On August 25 [1942] . . . Mala Weiss passed on a warning from the local [police] that a *rafle* [roundup of Jews] was planned that night. My father, having obtained a certificate from the local doctor that he was too ill to work and still in possession of his release papers from the [work] camp, decided he could remain home. I, of course, had to be hidden. No one imagined that the roundup might include women.

That evening, Mr. Granal [a neighbor] led me into their "cellar"; then up a ladder to the top of a story-high wooden wine vat, [then] over loose planks to the top of a concrete vat. There, among dusty discarded crates, he had arranged a hiding place for me.

After remaining atop the vat for perhaps a week, it was not Mr. Granal but his wife who came up the ladder one day. She . . . looked distraught. She must have struggled

Escaping German-occupied countries marked the beginning of escape for many Jews. Refugees on the run were constantly in dangerous situations. This map shows several escape routes from German-occupied territory.

long to get the terrible news off her chest. . . . "They took your [mother]."[1]

Alfred and his father received a letter from Mrs. Feldman, saying that she was in a work camp (named Rivesaltes), along with Alfred's two sisters. Shortly after this, a refugee-aid organization found a place for Alfred:

They told my father that I should come to Montpellier [a nearby town], where I would be given false identity papers and sent to a safe place. . . .

When I arrived in Montpellier, I left the bus stop quickly. "That is where they are watching," my father had warned me. "That is where they are checking identifications." . . . My father had told me to walk unhesitatingly down the avenue and to hail a cab as soon as I saw one. He had given me the address of a safe house to which the cab was to take me. I was expected, he had assured me, and they would pay my fare.

I was lucky. I spotted a taxi almost immediately, and it stopped when I hailed it. But as I got in, a man followed me, pushed me over, and closed the door. Just another passenger trying to share a scarce cab, I thought. When the cabbie asked for our destinations, I, innocently, gave mine first. I realized the terrible mistake I had made as soon as the other passenger said, "That is where I go, too." He had been following me, I realized. He was no common passenger. He was an undercover policeman. And I was leading him to the safe house, betraying all inside.

Alfred Feldman used a false identity card, like this one, while living in France to escape the Nazis. This false identity card belonged to Walter Karliner, who was hiding in southern France.

> As the cab rolled along, I risked a look
> at my pursuer. The man's eyes did not glint
> with the triumph of the sleuth cornering
> his quarry. They were downcast. He looked
> dispirited, as scared as I was. He must be
> a fellow refugee, I concluded, and we must
> have arrived on the same bus.[2]

That was only the beginning of Alfred Feldman's journey to survival. His mother and sisters were not so fortunate:

> Convoy 31, the train on whose transport
> list the names of my mother and sisters
> appear, left Paris on September 11, 1942,
> carrying over a thousand deportees. . . .
>   Their train arrived in Auschwitz on
> September 13. Of its passengers, the German
> jailers selected some to work; the rest
> were gassed immediately. Among those
> selected for work were seventy-eight women
> identified by the numbers 19530 through
> 19607 tattooed on their forearms. None
> survived. . . . I have not checked further.
> . . . I have gone far enough.[3]

The Killing Squads

Alfred Feldman did not know the fate of his mother and sisters until much later in his life. But Sally Baran's (Eisner) thirteen-year-old brother actually saw the bodies of their parents. They became victims of the Einsatzgruppen. These were the killing squads that followed the regular German army into the Soviet Union. Sally's parents' lives ended in a trench they were forced to dig for themselves.

This happened in a Ukrainian labor camp, when Sally and her thirteen-year-old brother were working in the fields:

It was in July 1943. We heard terrible sounds of shooting and shelling, coming from all over. We didn't know what was going on. . . . I was in the fields working when the Nazis surrounded the camp grounds, ordered everyone, including my parents, to dig a mass grave—their own. Then they were ordered to strip naked and line up. Then they were shot, one by one.

When the firing stopped and the Nazis had left, my brother, who was thirteen at the time, went back from the fields to see what happened. He saw our parents lying, with all the others, in that large ditch that became their grave. He immediately ran away. I lay in the fields terrified until it became completely dark. I went back to the camp the very next day and saw the mass grave and pools of blood, all over. . . . I started out in search of my brother. A day later, in a swampy part of the forest, I found him. We were both very frightened and utterly confused. He was practically speechless from shock.[4]

"He saw our parents lying, with all the others, in that large ditch that became their grave."

In their wanderings, Sally and her brother had many close calls. One of the closest happened when they were staying with a non-Jewish family, working for their room and board by helping with child care and farm chores:

One late afternoon, as dusk approached, my brother was chopping wood in front of the house and I was inside glancing out the window. I suddenly noticed three horsemen approaching. Someone had obviously told the Ukrainian police about our presence and now they were looking for us. . . .

I ran outside, grabbed my brother's hand pulled him inside and pushed him and myself under the . . . bed . . . to hide among the boots, shoes, and many other items that were stored there. We crept as far into the corner as we could, pressing our bodies against the wall. . . .

We heard the loud bang as they pushed open the door. . . . They started to search the house. . . . They thrust . . . bayonets under the bed, sweeping the floor with the blades, stabbing and jabbing into the dark and cluttered space, pulling out boots and shoes. I felt the knife point against my skin but we didn't make a sound. . . . When they were convinced that no one was under the bed, they went outside. . . .

We stayed under the bed for a long time after, afraid to come out. When the family came home and we told them what happened, they . . . told us to leave. It was a bitter cold winter night. We wandered about for days and finally ended up in a labour camp.[5]

Acting on Impulse

In Germany and Nazi-occupied territory, survival could depend on snap decisions and timely hunches. This was the case for teenager Florence Gittelman and her father:

[It was] just the two of us. . . . [Father]
. . . spoke fluently Russian, and he
had a profession. So he used to knock at
the peasant door and said if they need a
haircut, or a shave. And he said he has
to clean up his daughter. So one family—I
remember just like today, a nice peasant
family—they took me in. They gave me a
bath. She said, "I have nothing to wear
for you." . . . But she went into the pig
house—they . . . raised pigs—and they
took off the blankets from a pig and
she wrapped me around. And she gave me
a little kerchief to put on my head, and
she says, "Look, I would love to help you,
but I can't. You have to leave the house
immediately." But I cleaned up . . . and
they killed the lice from this little
outfit I wore. And we had to leave, so
we left . . . and this is what we did
for quite a few months. Walking at night—
walking daytime, sleeping in the woods
. . . and looking for the underground
people [Jewish freedom fighters in hiding].
Where are the underground people? . . .
[Father] knew if there [were] a lot of us,
somebody was going to tell on us from the
peasants; they gonna get us. Sure enough,
we joined some Jewish groups, and we went
into this house, and my father said . . .
"You know, . . . we have too many people.
Let's get out of here." And he grabbed me
and we left, we left this way. From [the
other side] the Germans were already there.
They killed everybody [in the hideout].[6]

Sometimes, these quick decisions could lead in surprising directions. For teenager Ruth Berkowicz, deciding to go to Vilna with friends led to a reunion with her father:

> [A] young man who was giving me Latin lessons came with his older brother—he was 18, his brother was 21—came to say good-bye to us. They said that they were leaving Warsaw [Poland]. It was somewhere around the middle of October. And . . . I decided on the spur of the moment I said to my mother, "Why don't I go with them? I'll contact our father. I'll tell him that we're alive and what happened and so on." And so . . . the next morning at five, six o'clock, I left. . . . It was all last minute and it was all based on the assumption that in two weeks I'll be back, or that the war will end very soon. There was no premonition . . . that we [would] never see each other again.[7]

"There was no premonition . . . that we [would] never see each other again."

Ruth knew that her father was supposed to be in Vilna, but she did not know how to contact him:

> I arrived at about four or five in the morning and I had to look for my father in a big city. . . . [The] only name that I [could] remember . . . our company in Warsaw . . . had a representative in Vilnius who used to do our buying. I remembered his name because I worked for

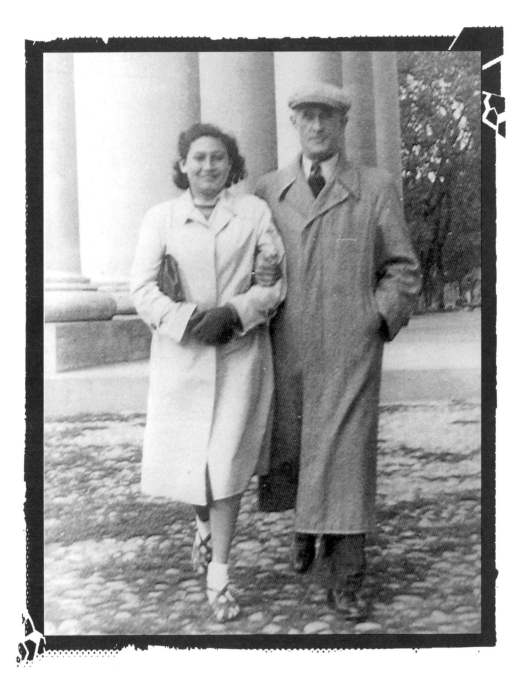

Ruth Berkowicz pictured with her uncle in Vilna, Lithuania, in September 1940. Ruth went to Vilna in search of her father.

a few months in my father's business while
waiting for my visa and my admission to
Zurich, to medical school. So I remembered
his name . . . at about seven o'clock
in the morning I went somewhere, I don't
know where, to a hotel, somewhere, to look
at the telephone book. And I found his
name. I called him up. I said, "I am
Ruth Berkowicz. I am the daughter of Leon
Berkowicz. . . . Did he by any chance
contact you because he's supposed to be in
Vilna?" And the guy said to me, "Wait ten
minutes and I will be with you." And he
came and he picked me up, . . . [and]
contacted . . . my father. That's the only
way. If I didn't have his name, I . . . I
mean it's . . . everything was just touch
and go, everything.[8]

Out of Norway

Margrit Rosenberg (Stenge) and her parents fled to Norway when
Hitler took over in Germany. They were safe enough there until
Germany conquered the country in 1940 and, all too soon, began
deporting Norwegian Jews to concentration camps. Margrit was
only thirteen at the time, but she felt the tension in the house. One
incident in particular stood out in her mind:

My father's depression and violent outbursts
became more frequent. We felt caught in
a trap with no way out. My fourteenth
birthday on December 27 [1942] was like any
other day, and when I complained that we
did not even have a small celebration, my
father completely lost his temper. I had

Ruth Berkowicz used this tan rucksack to carry her possessions during her travels. At the Polish border, German soldiers stole her belongings, but let her proceed. She traveled with this rucksack from Warsaw to Japan.

never seen him that furious and was really frightened when he lifted up a chair and threw it against the wall.[9]

Einar Wellen, a member of the Norwegian underground, had promised to get the family out of the country, but the deportations continued and Wellen did not come:

We had almost given up hope, when in the early morning hours of January 14, 1943 there was a knock on the door. Fearing the worst I opened the door. Relief surged through me when I recognized Einar Wellen with another young man, who turned out to be his friend Arne Myhrvold. Both were exhausted and frozen, because they had spent the night traveling, the last part on an open truck bed. The two young men wasted no time in telling us that everything was arranged for our escape and that we would be leaving early the following morning. They advised us how to dress and what to bring in our knapsacks. . . . We would travel by truck to a small place near Fagernes, where we would board a train headed for Oslo [Norway]. We would leave the train in a suburb of Oslo. A minister, recognizable by his clerical collar would meet us at the station and take us to his home where we would stay until the next transport to Sweden [a neutral country].

This plan sounded easy enough, but we all knew that danger would be lurking in every corner. The truck could easily be stopped for an inspection, and what was even more likely was, that we would be asked for identification papers on the train, but these were risks we had to take to save our lives. . . .

We left Rogne at dawn the following day. Our truck made it without incident in time for the train to Oslo. Einar and Arne traveled on the same train as we, but in a different compartment, and in fact we did not see them again. My father hid behind a newspaper, my mother and I tried to look as relaxed as possible. Not one word was spoken between us. By some miracle we were not asked for identification papers. When we reached the suburb of Oslo, where we were to meet the minister, we got off the train and looked anxiously around. But he was there, a car drove up immediately, and we were off to the minister's home. . . .

The next stop was a barn, where the Rosenbergs joined a group of other runaways. All of them boarded a truck for a two-hour drive that took them close to the Swedish border:

[We] were told that this was the end of our drive and that we would have to walk the

rest of the way to the Swedish border. A
guide would accompany us.

We walked through the snowy woods,
quickly and in absolute silence. Suddenly
a small cabin appeared as if from nowhere
with lights blinking through its windows.
And then we heard: "Welcome to Sweden,
come inside," and saw the outlines of two
Swedish soldiers coming towards us.

Our long odyssey, beginning in Oslo on
April 9, 1940 had ended.[10]

It was autumn 1945, and the Rosenbergs were going home.

One Small Ship

Twelve-year-old Evelyn Konrad and her family found refuge in
France until the French government declared all people from
Germany and Austria "enemy aliens." It did not matter that Evelyn
and her parents were Jewish, and therefore stripped of citizenship
in their native land; they were Austrians who spoke German as
their primary language. In wartime France, that was reason enough
for leaving: "By February 1940, my parents were desperate to get
out of France. Every day there were more news items in the papers
about internment of enemy aliens. All of us were frightened by the
. . . frequent air raids. Finally, my father got us a one-month
visitors' visa to Portugal."[11]

They ended up staying in Lisbon, Portugal, for three months.
That ended abruptly one night:

[M]y father picked me up out of my bed
while I was asleep, and carried me to a car
that took us to the pier. There, I heard my
mother say, in terror, "That small a ship?"

and heard my father say, "No, that one." I sneaked a peek, and next to the small ship I had seen my mother point to, I saw a tiny little ship. "But it's smaller than the little [boat] that runs up and down the Seine and never leaves Paris," she said. I squeezed my eyes shut, hearing all the good-byes between my parents and my Uncle Freddie, and I fell asleep again. . . .

I'm not sure whether it was the sun through the porthole or my mother's moaning that woke me up. On the bunk bed across from me in the cabin, I saw my mother writhe and heard her moan and beg to die. Her cheeks had lost their rosy color; they were all sunken and grayish-white. The door to the cabin opened, and my father staggered in, moving like someone who had had too much to drink.

> "I felt like throwing up, but I have never been able to throw up, and all that awful feeling stayed inside of me."

"What's wrong?" I asked, jumping down from my bunk bed.

"Don't you feel it?" my father asked. I shook my head. "Thank God," he said. . . .

The very first day out of the Azores [islands], it was pouring rain. In the morning when I woke up, my tummy felt as if I had left it behind in Santa Maria. I felt like throwing up, but I have never been able to throw up, and all that awful feeling stayed inside of me.

At night I did not sleep well, not because I was seasick, but because I was desperately worried about the German U-boats [submarines], that we had read so much about. . . . They were said to control the Atlantic, and no ship could escape them. So, during the day, I would go up on the deck and look out at the gray, rough ocean, searching for periscopes, so that I could warn the captain. . . . The only thing that reassured me about our ocean crossing was that we were carrying cork, and cork floats. I was a very strong swimmer and thought that if our boat was torpedoed, I would swim to one of the floating stacks of cork. I would pull my mother and father up with me, and we would float until we got to land or to a convoy from America. . . .

"At the end of the . . . day, the fog lifted, and in the distance . . . was New York harbor, with even the Statue of Liberty showing."

After nearly two weeks of seeing nothing but the gray sea . . . we came into a quiet zone of calm ocean, wrapped in a thick, thick fog. It seemed to me that [the boat] did not move at all. Every hour or so, she let out the mournful sound of her fog horn. I thought we were sitting ducks for the U-boats, and I prayed more often and more multi-lingually than ever before.

At the end of the second day, the fog lifted, and in the distance, but clearly visible, was New York harbor, with even the Statue of Liberty showing.[12]

Going to Shanghai

In Kaunas, Lithuania, Hanni Sondheimer had to get visas for her family's escape:

> When my father sent me to get the visas, I
> was a nervous wreck, and I was very angry,
> and he said, "You must, I can't lose one
> day's work because I'm lucky [to have a
> job]." It was awful. I must have stood
> there for many days. . . . When we were
> close to leaving my mother got sick and
> she had a fever and the doctor came to
> the house and gave her a prescription.
> She . . . said they couldn't go, and we
> forced her to go, we said, "We don't care.
> Whatever it takes." She had to come with
> us. . . . On the ship to Japan we slept
> like on top of each other, close, because
> the ship was very full.[13]

The family did not have to worry about Nazis in Asia, but they did face hardship: "In [1943] . . . we were put into a ghetto [in Japanese-occupied Shanghai, China]. We had no toilets; we built our own toilet on a roof garden, and every morning they'd empty the pot, take it downstairs in the alley and clean it, put the stuff in a little wagon, it was bad."[14]

In 1940, eighteen-year-old Ruth Berkowicz and her father made their way from Vilna, Lithuania, to Japan, and from there were sent to Japanese-occupied Shanghai, China, by an even more complicated route:

> Well, when the first people started going
> across to . . . Japan . . . we applied for
> an exit visa. You . . . not only [needed] a

Many Jews, like Hanni Sondheimer, fled to Shanghai, China, during the Holocaust. A Jewish family established this leather goods factory in Shanghai.

transit visa to Japan—you know the transit
visa was only for ten days—but . . . also
had to get an exit visa from the Soviets.
And so . . . we applied for exit. . . .
There was a room . . . where the man . . .
read a list of people who were getting
exit visas that day. And one day . . . they
mentioned my name, without my father. So
I got very upset. I didn't want to go by
myself across the Soviet Union and leave my
father behind. . . . It was no good. And so
. . . I came home and I said to my father,
"They read my name. They didn't read your
name." And my father said, " . . . Ruthka,
you have to go. You are 18 years old.
You are young. You have your whole life
ahead of you. You've got to go." And so
I decided to go. . . . Two weeks later my
father came.[15]

Help Along the Way

Even in the desperate times of the Holocaust, fugitives occasionally
received kindness from others. Ten-year-old Johanna Gerechter
and her parents found a safe haven in Italy, although it supported
Germany in the war. The Gerechters left Germany with ten marks
per person. By the time they arrived in Bologna, Italy, they had
used all their money:

[We] stood on the platform in Bologna and
really didn't know where to turn. To our
great surprise . . . there were Italian
students who . . . were organized by the
Jewish community of Italy. . . . [T]hese
students had made it their business to be

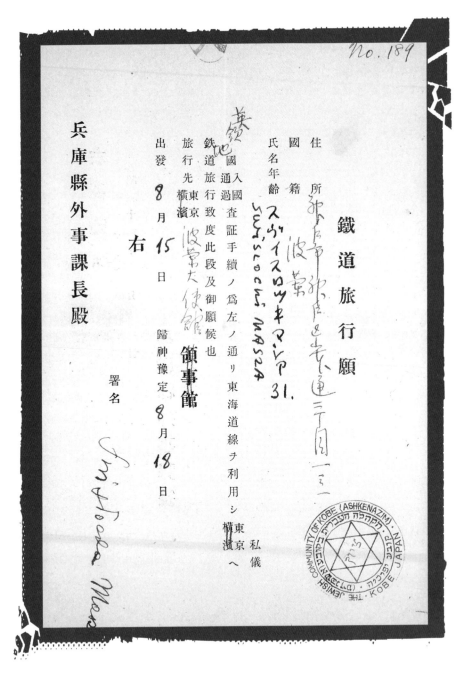

Ruth Berkowicz and her father traveled from Vilna to Japan, and then they were sent to Shanghai, China. This is a Japanese railway permit issued to a Jewish refugee traveling through Japan.

there and . . . receive German or other
immigrants that were fleeing Germany. Well,
I remember two students taking us in hand,
taking us to a beautiful, beautiful hotel,
and caring for us for an entire week until
we were able to receive money from our
relatives in America.[16]

Some Jews found help from complete strangers. The quick
thinking of a woman that Erika Eckstut had never met rescued her
from the clutches of a German soldier. It happened when Erika
was posing as a Gentile in order to buy food outside the ghetto:

I saw a German soldier beating a man on
the ground who was bleeding. The soldier
was on crutches and his chest was full
of decorations. He stood on one of the
crutches and with the other he beat the
man. I approached the soldier and in my
perfect German lectured him on how wrong
he was to beat a man who did not defend
himself. As I was busy giving my lecture,
people stood around listening. All of a
sudden a policeman touched my arm and said,
"That will be enough little girl; let's
go home."

At that moment I realized, "I can't go
home. If I take him to the ghetto my whole
family will be killed." So I took him to
an opera singer who lived not far from the
ghetto. She was, of course, a gentile. When
we arrived at the door and rang the bell a
beautiful lady opened the door and I said,
"Mama." The policeman at the same time
said, "Is this your daughter, Madame?" She
ignored him, and pointing a finger at me,

Johanna Gerechter washing dishes outdoors in Shkoset, Albania, on August 6, 1942. The Gerechter family eventually immigrated to the United States.

she said: "I told you once, I told you twice, home and homework." The policeman in the meantime kept repeating his question, and, in desperation, she started hitting me in the face. It was so painful that I hardly cared what happened at this point. Then, as if in a dream, I heard the policeman saying, "Keep her, keep her, just stop hitting her." After the policeman left, she took me inside, gave me a hug, and asked, "Are you from the ghetto?"

I have forgotten so many names from during the Holocaust, but I still remember her.[17]

In a similar incident, Roza Weintraub's father saved a fellow Jew he happened to see on the train:

Since [Roza's father] went by train a lot, he knew all the officials. He saw this refugee standing in the door, without hope. He could see that the man was a Jew, [and] he said: "What's the problem?" The man said: "I have only one option left—to jump off the train." He came from Danzig, and wanted to reach Vilna. His family was in Vilna. He had earlier been caught and sent back to Germany. So father bumped him, hugged him, started to kiss him and said: "Oh, it's good to see you, my brother, I am very happy to see you." Father took some money from his pocket, put some Lits [Lithuanian currency] into this Gendarme's pocket, and rescued the Jew. Later there was a recurrent thought. When I was in Russia and people were nice to me, I said

that's because of father, because he had
helped the refugees a lot. That's the thing
I had to go back for.[18]

These spontaneous rescues took courage, daring, and an ability to think fast in dangerous situations. Though these rescues did occur, they were not common; the Nazis had seen to that. In the occupied nations, the penalty for helping Jews was death. Even well-meaning people were often too afraid to help.

Jewish fugitives learned to live with this. They became wary of strangers and were careful not to reveal too much about themselves. Many made a point of not staying too long in any one place. They lived in constant fear of recognition and capture. Many fugitives who eventually found sanctuary faced a new challenge: learning to live as strangers in an unknown land, surrounded by cultures they did not understand. For young people who missed their homes and families, adjusting to this life was an act of courage.

Chapter Six

FIGHTING BACK

On June 22, 1941, German troops invaded the Soviet Union. "Operation Barbarossa," as Hitler called it, was supposed to bring the Soviets to their knees in a matter of months, or even weeks. Things did not work out that way. At first, Soviet defenses crumbled under the fierce Nazi onslaught, but the Red Army never stopped fighting back. In time, the limitation of Hitler's blitzkrieg began to show. It was not suited to long, drawn-out warfare. As their military fortunes declined, the Nazis ran short of troops, weaponry, and supplies. In spite of this, Hitler refused to cut back on the "final solution"—the Nazi-coordinated plan to murder all the Jews of Europe.

While Germany floundered on the battlefield, the trains to the death camps kept running and the Nazis kept them filled. Day and night, the trains transported Jews from ghettos to killing centers with gas chambers and huge brick ovens—crematoria—to burn the bodies.

A Call for Resistance

On New Year's Eve 1941, about 150 young activists gathered in the Vilna (Lithuania) ghetto. Any large gathering of Jews was likely to trigger Nazi suspicion, so they disguised the meeting as a New Year's Eve party. Their real purpose was to unite different youth groups into a fighting force. Abba Kovner, one of the most

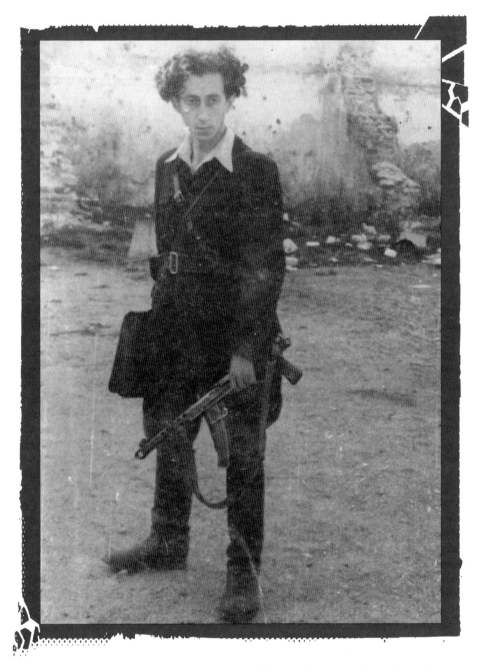

Abba Kovner holding a weapon in Vilna after the city fell to the Soviet army in July 1944. Kovner was a leader of the resistance in the Vilna ghetto and became a partisan fighter.

militant leaders in the Vilna ghetto, delivered an impassioned call
to revolt:

> Let us not go like sheep to the slaughter,
> Jewish youth! Do not believe those who are
> deceiving you. Out of 80,000 Jews of the
> Jerusalem of Lithuania (Vilna), only 20,000
> remain. In front of your eyes our parents,
> our brothers and our sisters are being torn
> away from us. Where are the hundreds of men
> who were snatched away for labor by the
> Lithuanian kidnappers? Where are those naked
> women who were taken away on the horror-night
> of the provocation? Where are those Jews
> of the Day of Atonement? And where are our
> brothers of the second ghetto? Anyone who
> is taken out through the gates of the ghetto,
> will never return. All roads of the ghetto
> lead to Ponary [a killing field outside
> of Vilna], and Ponary means death. Oh,
> despairing people—tear this deception
> away from your eyes. Your children, your
> husbands, your wives—are no longer alive—
> Ponary is not a labor camp. Everyone there
> is shot. Hitler aimed at destroying the Jews
> of Europe. It turned out to be the fate of
> the Jews of Lithuania to be the first. Let
> us not go like sheep to the slaughter. It
> is true that we are weak, lacking protection,
> but the only reply to a murderer is resis-
> tance. Brothers, it is better to die as free
> fighters than to live at the mercy of killers.
> Resist, resist, to our last breath.[1]

The reading had its intended effect. On the eve of 1942,
Abba Kovner laid the foundation for what would become the

Lithuanian police herd a column of Jews to be murdered in the Ponary forest. During Abba Kovner's speech, he urged people to remember what happened at Ponary. Lithuanian police, who were Nazi collaborators, executed thousands of Jews at this site.

United Partisans Organization or FPO (Lithuanian initials). On September 1, 1943, the FPO attacked German troops who had come into the ghetto to seize two thousand Jews. The partisans attacked but the ghetto leadership did not stand behind them. Abba Kovner realized that fighting inside the ghetto would be useless, so the partisans escaped through the sewers and established a base of operation in the Rudnicki forest. From there, they committed many acts of sabotage against German forces.

Fighting Back

Armed resistance was not the only way of fighting back. Jews who could not take up arms found other ways to defy the Nazis. Young children risked their lives smuggling food to starving people in the ghettos. Jews of all ages ignored Nazi directives to keep their traditions alive: rabbis gathered people for Sabbath services; teachers held classes in bunkers and basements; diarists, historians, and social commentators recorded their experiences for posterity. Jews from all walks of life created hiding places, made daring escapes, and took life-or-death risks in the struggle for survival.

Eleven-year-old Renata Eisen and her mother heard no stirring speech and planned no brave battle with the Nazis. But they realized their survival depended upon taking great risks. Renata remembered her mother confronting officials to improve their chances of survival:

```
From the fall of 1941 and for the next two
years, I lived in Italy under Mussolini.
While the Italian government was officially
fascist and allied with Germany, the
Italian people my family and I encountered
```

were exceptionally warm, generous and hospitable. We were the "poveri stranieri," poor foreigners, so we were treated with particular kindness.

After we had been about five months in Italy, my mother was able to convince the Italian authorities to relocate my father and brother [from Zagreb, Yugoslavia] . . . to the town in Northern Italy to which we had been assigned. . . .

In the same way she had foreseen other dangers, my mother recognized the threat that German troops might enter Northern Italy and deport the Jews there to concentration camps. This did happen in 1943. But by that time we had again been relocated—once more thanks to my mother's persistent requests to the Italian authorities—to a town near the Alps, straddling the border with Switzerland.

When the Germans invaded Italy, my family and I climbed those formidable mountains. After days of hiking, we reached a Swiss border point. The Swiss were refusing entry to refugees, but once again my mother's survival instinct saved our lives. She simply told the guards that the Germans would certainly kill us if we went back, and since we were physically drained we were not going to move from where we were. They were free to shoot us themselves, she told them. We lay down on the spot. Eventually, an officer came and escorted us into the interior of the country.[2]

The Eisens lived out the rest of the war in Switzerland.

Renata Eisen and her family escaped Italy by trekking over the Alps mountains after the German invasion. Jewish refugees escaping over the Alps into Italy are shown in this photo.

Jumping Off the Death Train

Eva Galler was seventeen when the Nazis began rounding up Jews in the ghetto of Lubaczow, Poland:

> Beginning on January 4, 1943, the Gestapo and the Polish and Ukrainian police started to chase all the Jews out from their houses. The deportation took several days. People ran and hid. The Jewish police helped to find the people in hiding. They had been promised that they would stay alive if they cooperated.
>
> We knew where we were going. A boy from our town had been deported to Belzec camp. He escaped and came back to our town. He told us that Belzec had a crematorium. Deportation trains from other cities had passed by our city and people had thrown out notes. These notes were picked up by the men forced to work there. The notes said, "Don't take anything with you, just water."
>
> They took us to a cattle train. People started to run away from the train, but they were shot. Once on the train we had to stand because there was no room to sit down. A boy tore the barbed wires from the train window. The young people started to jump out of the window. Many jumped. The SS on the rooftop of the train shot at them with rifles. My father told us, the oldest three, "Run, run—maybe you will stay alive. We will stay here with the small children because even if they get out, they will not be able to survive." . . .

My brother Berele jumped out, then my sister Hannah, and then I jumped out. The SS men shot at us. I landed in a snowbank. The bullets did not hit me. When I did not hear anything anymore, I went back to find my brother and my sister. I found them dead. My brother Berele was 15. My sister Hannah was 16. I was 17.[3]

The next day, Eva made her way through the woods to the train station in the city of Jaroslaw:

At that time it was thought that there were partisans in the woods. People were afraid to go in the woods, but I was not afraid. I was walking in the deep snow, and in the evening I came to the station. . . .

I bought a ticket for Cracow. I figured that Cracow was a big city with a big Jewish community. Maybe the ghetto would still be there. In the train station I saw [someone I knew]. . . . I was frightened that she might recognize me. I kept walking around the block until the train came. Then I got on the train. This was another situation. I did not have any documents.

. . . There were identification checks on the train. Every station I would move to another wagon.

In Cracow I spent two days and two nights living in the train station.

> "I went back to find my brother and my sister. I found them dead. My brother Berele was 15. My sister Hannah was 16. I was 17."

Jews resisted the Nazis in many ways during the Holocaust. One way was by writing a diary. This illustrated diary entry written in a Swiss refugee camp describes Bruna Cases' (an Italian Jewish refugee) escape over the Alps to Switzerland.

There was a curfew at night because of the war. People who came into the city late had to stay in the train station until morning, so there were always a lot of people there. I moved around a lot so people would not recognize me, from one bench to another, from one room to another. It was a big station. But I did not have any money, and I did not have any bread. I had never been to Cracow before. . . . I did not see anybody with an armband, and I was scared to ask someone where the ghetto was.

I walked and walked. I was hungry. . . . I came to a market place, a farmers' market. I could hear running. They closed up the market place and took all the young people aside. I could hear the girls and boys talking. They were catching boys and girls and sending them to work in Germany. Nobody would go work freely in Germany; they had to use force. This was how they rounded up the people. I was very glad that I was caught with those people. I was caught as a Gentile and not as a Jew. . . . I assumed the identity of a Polish girl, Katarzyna Czuchowska, a name I made up.[4]

As Katarzyna, Eva survived the war years working on a farm in Austria.

Escape From the Warsaw Ghetto

In the Warsaw Ghetto, a group of Jewish teenagers and young adults formed the Jewish Fighting Organization (ZOB, the Polish initials). They had fought a limited action battle against the Nazis in January 1943, perhaps forcing the Nazis to regroup. Some three months later, the Nazis came in force, and the fighters faced a battle they could neither delay nor win. It began on April 19, 1943, when German troops came to destroy the ghetto and everyone in it.

"In this situation . . . it was only a question of time until we would all be buried alive under the debris."

The ZOB had been preparing for this moment. Instead of allowing the Nazis to control them, they fought back with pistols, rifles, and homemade bombs. For nearly a month, they held off destruction and inflicted significant losses on the enemy. The battle ended with the ghetto in flames. A few survivors did escape to the non-Jewish side of the city, while others became trapped in underground bunkers within the still-burning ghetto.

Simha Rotem (code name Kazik) was part of a plan to rescue as many fighters as possible:

> After eleven or twelve days of battle . . . the Germans continued destroying the Ghetto from outside, with artillery bombardments and air attacks; finally, sappers [explosives experts] were sent to set fires and explode every cellar and bunker. In this situation . . . it was only a question of time until we would all be buried alive under the debris. The command staff therefore decided to find a way to rescue the fighters who could still be saved so they could continue fighting the Germans under other conditions.[5]

The partisans decided to go through the elaborate sewer system beneath the streets of Warsaw. Gradually a plan to get the fighters out of the Ghetto took shape. "We needed an exit base where we could descend into the sewers; a guide from the sewer workers; and transportation to take the fighters . . . to the forest, where they would join a group of comrades who had left the Ghetto . . . and had been living in the forest since the end of April."[6]

The partisan escape through the sewers of Warsaw has become an enduring image of courage in the face of impossible odds. This was not the case immediately after the war as Simha Rotem discovered when he immigrated to Palestine (present-day Israel):

> A harsh and disappointing reality awaited me [there].
>
> My meeting with Melekh Neustadt, one of the first people I met here, concerned the fighters of the Warsaw Ghetto. I was interrogated about everyone who had been killed, but I was never asked, even remotely, about those who had survived.
>
> In almost every meeting with people in Eretz Israel, the question came up, "How did you survive?" It was asked again and again, and not always in the most delicate way. I had the feeling that I was guilty for surviving. This was why, even after I learned Hebrew, I didn't talk very much. . . . I preferred not to tell about myself and where I had spent the war years.[7]

Survivor guilt was common among Jews who survived while six million other Jews had perished. Probing questions only made matters worse. Rather than deal with them, many young survivors became reluctant to talk about their wartime experiences.

As the truth emerged through newsreels, photographs, diaries, and eyewitness accounts, a stunned world began to realize that the unthinkable was true: the ghettos, the killing fields, the cattle cars, the death camps, the six million Jewish victims and the millions of other victims—all of it. In view of these facts, when young survivors finally did tell their stories, people wanted to listen.

Chapter Seven

LUCK AND SURVIVAL

By the spring of 1945, Hitler could no longer doubt that Germany was losing the war. The Soviets were closing from the east and the British and Americans from the west. In a desperate attempt to escape the Allies, guards at many camps rounded up prisoners who could still walk and fled with them toward the interior of Germany. These became known as "death marches." As many as 15,000 Jews died on the "death march" from Auschwitz.[1]

Germans on the Run

Even before the marches started, sixteen-year-old Fritzie Weiss and fellow prisoners at Auschwitz sensed that the war was coming to an end:

> [W]e knew because of the bombings and we knew because of the way the German soldiers were pushing us and pulling us already and emptying the camps. . . . They took us all and put us together, all of the people from camps, and they had us march through towns and through fields. They didn't know where to put us anymore and they didn't know what to do with us and there was no food because the Germans were losing the war. Oftentimes as they marched us through a town, a window would open and a shutter would open and

either a potato or a loaf of bread would come flying out and the shutter would close after. And we would all pounce on this potato or . . . whatever this piece of food was that came at us. And of course [the guards] would shoot at us, but we didn't care at that point because we were hungry. The streets were literally covered with bodies as we marched. We would pass . . . body after body after body, people that were dropping dead from hunger, from disease, from dysentery, because they did not have the strength or because they gave up.[2]

The Holocaust took away Sam Itzkowitz's youth. He was fourteen when the war started and twenty when it ended. Sam was in Dachau when the guards and staff rounded up prisoners and marched them toward the Bavarian Alps:

These boots were worn by a female Jewish prisoner, Ala Brand, in Auschwitz and on a death march. Thousands of Jews died on the death marches at the end of the Holocaust.

Till today I don't know what the reason was. Either they wanted to destroy us . . . in those mountains or they were going to trade us off through Switzerland. There was the death march. Well, I was already so weak that I could

barely walk. That march . . . took about
. . . ten days to two weeks. Snow in the
daytime, snow at night. . . . And we had to
sleep outside . . . they always camped us
out somewhere in an open field. And we just
huddled together like animals . . . in the
wilderness. And tried to, just tried to
stay alive. And on top of it, we saw planes
coming over us. . . . And we were praying,
hoping . . . "Come on, drop them, get it
over with." Well I don't know. I think the
pilots saw that we were prisoners and they
dropped bombs all around us, but never on
us. See we were wearing those striped . . .
uniforms. And they didn't fly too high to
start with because they were bombing in the
daytime. So probably this is the only thing
that saved us.[3]

Call It Luck

Sam Itzkowitz's story focuses on circumstances beyond his control; in other words, luck. This theme appears often in survivor testimony. Survivors made it clear that they were not smarter, more courageous, or more deserving than those who died. They "just happened" to run away in the nick of time, find helpers when they needed them most, or were out of reach when the Nazis were filling the death camps.

Decades after surviving the war as a teenager, Alexander Schenker explained his ideas about luck:

I am convinced now that in life everything
is a question of luck. We were immensely
lucky in all kinds of ways throughout

This group of female survivors trudges through the snow after the liberation of Auschwitz. Many Holocaust survivors faced new problems after liberation, such as dealing with guilt and finding a new home.

the war. I mean considering the place where
we found ourselves, and that is at the very
[center] . . . of this horror, to get out
of it in the shape in which we got out of
it took an immense amount of luck. And . . .
you know luck is really a question of
coincidence. You happen . . . to turn left
when you have a choice to go straight and
to go right. You don't know . . . why you
are going left, and yet to turn left turns
out to be the lucky [choice].[4]

A Strange Kind of Luck

Ten-year-old Thomas Buergenthal had his own definition of
luck—it was anything that kept him alive, however terrible the
event itself might be. By that standard, losing several toes to frost-
bite in the brutal winter of 1945 was a stroke of luck. Thomas was
laid up at Sachsenhausen (a camp near Berlin) when the Germans
decided to run. On April 21, 1945, they grabbed every prisoner
who could still walk and fled toward the mountains. Thomas was
among the prisoners left behind in the so-called hospital ward.
This was actually the last stop before the gas chambers.

When the Germans fled they did not have time to use the gas,
so the hospital inmates expected to be shot in their beds. Decades
later, Thomas recalled that fateful day:

I remember . . . when people lined up,
and then it became extremely quiet, and
you couldn't hear anything. . . . And we
waited, basically on the assumption that
any minute now [the Germans] would come in.
Nothing happened. . . . I had a crutch and

> I could move. . . . [So] I went out to
> look, because [of] all this silence. And
> . . . the camp was empty . . . the Germans
> had left. . . . By then, you could hear
> already the rumbling of artillery . . . in
> the background. And there wasn't a soul to
> be seen. . . . Eventually . . . the gates
> swung open, and . . . Russian troops came
> in. And they began ringing . . . the camp
> bell to say that we were free.[5]

The Soviets came into camp on April 22, just one day after the Germans left. The prisoners on the death march were not rescued for another thirteen days; time enough for hundreds more to die. Thomas might well have been among them.

"And they began ringing . . . the camp bell to say that we were free."

Thomas did not feel guilty for his near-miraculous survival, though he knew survivors who carried a burden of guilt because they had lived while so many others did not:

> I have never experienced these [guilt]
> feelings. I don't know why, but if I were
> to speculate, I would attribute their
> absence to the instinctive belief of
> children in their own immortality and their
> entitlement to live. It may also be that
> since I attributed my survival to sheer
> luck, I came to view survival and non-
> survival as a game of chance over which
> I had no control and was, therefore, not
> responsible for the outcome.[6]

Regardless of how they lived through the Holocaust, young survivors faced hard times after the war. Thousands had no place to go and no one to care for them. The Nazis had destroyed their homes and killed their families. After enduring the unthinkable, they had to muster the courage for yet another task—learning to live with the past while building a future. Those who survived served notice that the Nazis not only lost the war, but also failed to carry out their "final solution to the Jewish question."

TIMELINE

1938

July 6–15—Evian Conference on German-Jewish refugees.

November 9–10—*Kristallnacht*; mass violence and vandalism against Jews in Germany.

December 1–September 1, 1939—The *Kindertransport* program takes many Jewish children to safety in England.

1939

May 13–June 17—Voyage of the SS *St. Louis* from Europe to Cuba and back again.

September 1—Germany invades Poland.

September 27—Warsaw surrenders to Germany.

1940

April 9—Germany invades Denmark and Norway.

May 10—Germany invades Holland, Belgium, and France.

October 12—Warsaw ghetto established.

November 16—Warsaw ghetto sealed off; Jews not allowed to leave.

1941

June 22—Germany invades Soviet Union; *Einsatzgruppen* death squads begin wholesale slaughter of Jews.

July 31—SS officer Reinhard Heydrich ordered to "solve the Jewish problem by means of emigration and evacuation."

October 23—Jews forbidden to emigrate from the German Reich (Empire).

1942

January 20—Wannsee conference coordinates the "final solution to the Jewish question."

1943

April 19–May 16—Warsaw ghetto uprising.

June 21—SS orders complete destruction of all ghettos in Poland.

1944

March 19—Germany invades Hungary and begins deporting Jews to camps.

1945

January—Allies advance on German positions; death marches begin.

May 8—Germany surrenders unconditionally to the Allies.

CHAPTER NOTES

Chapter 1. Alicia's Journey

1. Alicia Appleman-Jurman, *Alicia: My Story* (New York: Bantam Books, paperback edition, 1989), p. 13.
2. Ibid., p. 95.
3. Ibid., p. 139.
4. Ibid., p. 174.
5. Ibid., p. 180.
6. Ibid., p. 181.

Chapter 2. The Right Time to Go

1. Liane Reif-Lehrer, *Oral History Interview*, United States Holocaust Memorial Museum (USHMM) Archives, RG-50.233*0108.
2. "Kristallnacht Order: November 10, 1938," Jewish Virtual Library, 2009, <http://www.jewishvirtuallibrary.org/jsource/Holocaust/kristallnacht_order.html> (May 24, 2008).
3. "Kristallnacht," Jewish Virtual Library, 2009, <http://www.jewishvirtual library.org/jsource/Holocaust/kristallnacht.html> (May 24, 2008).
4. Fred Ederer, *Survivor Testimonies*, USHMM Archives, RG-01.087.
5. Gerda Feldman, *Oral History*, USHMM Archives, RG-50.030*0429.
6. Kazik (Simha Rotem), *Memoirs of a Warsaw Ghetto Fighter* (New Haven, Conn.: Yale University Press. 1994), p. 10.
7. Yitzhak Zuckerman, *A Surplus of Memory: Chronicle of the Warsaw Ghetto Uprising* (Berkeley, Calif.: University of California Press, 1993), p. 3.
8. Charlene Schiff (Shulamit Perlmutter), "The Haystack—1942," USHMM, 2002, <http://www.ushmm.org/remembrance/survivoraffairs/memory/detail.php?content=schiff> (May 12, 2009).

Chapter 3. The Search for Refuge

1. Ursula Bacon, *Shanghai Diary: A Young Girl's Journey from Hitler's Hate to War-Torn China* (Milwaukie, Ore.: M Press, 2004), pp. 13–14
2. Ibid., p. 13.
3. "Leo Melamed: Family Odyssey," United States Holocaust Memorial

Museum: Flight and Rescue, n.d., <http://www.ushmm.org/museum/exhibit/online/flight_rescue/search_results.php?type=2&q=&object_type=Video> (May 23, 2008).

4. Ibid.

5. Ibid.

6. Eva Rappoport Edmands, "Describes packing to leave Vienna for France in 1938," Personal Histories: Refugees, Unites States Holocaust Memorial Museum, n.d., <http://www.ushmm.org/museum/exhibit/online/phistories/viewmedia/phi_fset.php?MediaId=2893> (May 28, 2008).

7. Edith Schleissner Nathan, "A Survivor From Czechoslovakia," Hunter College H.S. Survivors, © 2000, <http://business.virgin.net/er.kugler/hchs/hchs_accounts2.htm> (May 28, 2008).

8. Ibid.

9. Ibid.

10. Ibid.

11. Evelyn Konrad, "Dodging U-boats Crossing the Atlantic," Hunter College H.S. Holocaust Survivors, © 2000, <http://business.virgin.net/er.kugler/hchs/hchs_accounts6.htm> (May 29, 2008).

12. Ibid.

13. Rosa Weintraub, "Memoirs of Roza Weintraub—Her Oral History Prepared at Kibbutz Nir David—26.6.1985," n.d., <http://www.shtetlinks.jewishgen.org/kibart/rozamem.html> (May 18, 2009).

14. Ibid.

15. Lucille Szepsenwol Camhi, "Family Odyssey," USHMM online exhibit, n.d., <http://www.ushmm.org/museum/exhibit/online/flight_rescue/search_results.php?type=2&q=&object_type=Video Accessed> (May 23, 2008).

16. Ibid.

17. Ibid.

Chapter 4. Two Journeys

1. "Timeline of Dachau," Jewish Virtual Library, 2009, <http://www.jewishvirtuallibrary.org/jsource/Holocaust/dachautime.html> (April 20, 2009).

2. Alice Eberstarkova Masters, *Oral History Transcript*, United States Holocaust Memorial Museum (USHMM) Archives, RG-50.030*0360.

3. Ibid.

4. Norbert Wollheim "Kindertransport. 1938–1940," USHMM, n.d., <http://www.ushmm.org/wlc/media_oi.php?lang=en&ModuleId=10005260&MediaId=2489> (June 26, 2008).

5. "The Kindertransports: Paul M. Cohn," A History of the Jews in Hamburg, n.d., <http://www1.uni-hamburg.de/rz3a035//kindertransport.html> (June 26, 2008).

6. Alice (Ebostarkova) Masters, "Kindertransport. 1938–1940," n.d., <http://www.ushmm.org/wlc/media_oi.php?lang=en&ModuleId=10005260&MediaId=2480> (May 12, 2009).

7. Ibid.

8. Inge Sachs Rosenthal, *Oral History Interview*, USHMM Archives, RG-50.030*0389.

9. Ibid.

10. Gerda Feldman, *Oral History*, USHMM Archives, RG-50.030*0429.

11. Gerda Blachmann Wilchfort, *Oral History Interview*, USHMM Archives, RG-50.030*0251.

12. Feldman.

13. Blachmann Wilchfort.

14. Feldman.

Chapter 5. One Step Ahead of Disaster

1. Alfred Feldman and Susan Zuccotti, *One Step Ahead: A Jewish Fugitive in Hitler's Europe* (Carbondale, Ill.: Southern Illinois University Press), pp. 97–98.

2. Ibid., p. 102.

3. Ibid., p. 101.

4. Sally Eisner, "Personal Reflections—In Hiding," Women and the Holocaust, © 2001, <http://www3.sympatico.ca/mighty1/personal/sally.htm> (June 3, 2008).

5. Ibid.

6. Florence Gittelman Eisen, *Oral History Interview*, United States Holocaust Memorial Museum (USHMM) Archives, RG-50.030*0260.

7. Ruth Berkowicz (Segal), "Flight and Rescue," USHMM, n.d., <http://www.ushmm.org/museum/exhibit/online/flight_rescue/search_results.php?type=2&q=&object_type=Video> (June 29, 2008).

8. Ruth Berkowicz Segal, "Testimony," USHMM, n.d., <http://www.ushmm.org/lcmedia/viewer/wlc/testimony.php?RefId=RSF0976F> (May 12, 2009).

9. Margrit Rosenberg Stenge, "Margrit's Story: Narrow Escape to and From Norway," The Concordia University Chair in Canadian Jewish Studies and The Montreal Institute for Genocide and Human Rights Studies, 2004, <http://migs.concordia.ca/memoirs/margit_rosenberg_stenge/margrit_rosenberg_stenge_02.htm> (June 8, 2008).

10. Ibid.

11. Evelyn Konrad, "Dodging U-boats Crossing the Atlantic," Hunter College H.S. Holocaust Survivors, © 2000, <http://business.virgin.net/er.kugler/hchs/hchs_accounts6.htm> (May 29, 2008).

12. Ibid.

13. Hanni Sondheimer Vogelweid, "Flight and Rescue," USHMM, n.d., <http://www.ushmm.org/museum/exhibit/online/flight_rescue/search_results.php?type=3&q=&survivors=Hanni%20Sondheimer%20Vogelweid:%20Family%20Odyssey> (July 2, 2008).

14. Ibid.

15. Ruth Berkowicz Segal.

16. Johanna Gerechter Neumann, "Survivor Volunteers," USHMM, n.d., <http://www.ushmm.org/remembrance/survivoraffairs/meet/view_media.php?content=neumann&type=interview> (June 12, 2008).

17. Erika Eckstut (Neuman), "Lasting Memory," USHMM, n.d., <http://www.ushmm.org/remembrance/survivoraffairs/memory/detail.php?content=eckstut#01-memory.txt> (May 2, 2008).

18. Rosa Weintraub, "Memoirs of Roza Weintraub—Her Oral History Prepared at Kibbutz Nir David—26.6.1985," n.d., <http://www.shtetlinks.jewishgen.org/kibart/rozamem.html> (May 18, 2009).

Chapter 6. Fighting Back

1. Abba Kovner, "The First Call: Manifesto of Jewish Resistance by Abba Kovner," Holocaust Survivors.org, © 1999–2009, <http://www.holocaustsurvivors.org/data.show.php?di=record&da=texts&ke=1> (June 28, 2008).

2. Renata Eisen, "Personal Reflections—In Hiding," Woman and the Holocaust, © 2001, <http://www3.sympatico.ca/mighty1/personal/renata.htm> (May 25, 2008).

3. "Survivor Stories: Eva Galler," Holocaust Survivors, © 1999–2000, <http://www.holocaustsurvivors.org/cgi-bin/data.show.pl?di=record&da=survivors&ke=6> (June 26, 2008).

4. Ibid.

5. Kazik (Simha Rotem), *Memoirs of a Warsaw Ghetto Fighter* (New Haven Conn.: Yale University Press, 1994), p. 41.

6. Ibid., p. 49.

7. Ibid., pp. 152–153.

Chapter 7. Luck and Survival

1. "Auschwitz," United States Holocaust Memorial Museum (USHMM), May 4, 2009, <http://www.ushmm.org/wlc/article.php?ModuleId= 10005189> (May 12, 2009).

2. Fritzie Weiss Fritzshall, "Describes the Death March from Auschwitz," United States Holocaust Memorial Museum (USHMM), n.d., <https:// secure.ushmm.org/museum/exhibit/online/phistories/viewmedia/phi_fset .php?MediaId=2863> (July 1, 2008).

3. Sam Itzkowitz, "Describes a death march from Landsberg, a subcamp of Dachau, to the Bavarian Alps," USHMM, n.d., <http://www.ushmm.org/ lcmedia/viewer/wlc/testimony.php?RefId=SIDO286M> (July 7, 2008).

4. Alexander Schenker, "Describes how he is convinced now that in life everything is a question of luck," USHMM, n.d., <http://www.ushmm. org/lcmedia/viewer/wlc/testimony.php?RefId=SIDO286M> (July 3, 2008).

5. Thomas Buergenthal, "Describes the Liberation of the Sachsenhausen camp," 1990 Interview, USHMM, n.d., <http://www.ushmm.org/wlc/ media_oi.php?lang=en&ModuleId=10006193&MediaId=2611> (May 2, 2009).

6. Thomas Buergenthal, *A Lucky Child: A Memoir of Surviving Auschwitz as a Young Boy* (New York: Little, Brown and Company, 2009), p. 209.

GLOSSARY

antisemitism—Fear and hatred of Jews.

blitzkrieg—"Lightning war" (German).

bunker—An underground fortification or hiding place.

chancellor—Head of state in a parliamentary government.

concentration camp—A prison for civilians, political prisoners, and enemy aliens, including Jews.

death camp—A facility designed for mass murder, with gas chambers and crematory ovens.

death march—Forced evacuation of Jewish prisoners by Germans fleeing Allied troops.

Einsatzgruppen—German killing squads that operated in the Soviet Union after the German invasion in June 1941.

emigrate—To leave one country and settle in another.

eretz Israel—The land of Israel (Hebrew).

"final solution"—Nazi term for the coordinated plan for extermination of the Jewish people.

Gentile—A non-Jewish person.

Gestapo (*Geheimestaatspolizei*)—Internal security police known for terrorist methods against persons suspected of treason or disloyalty to Nazi Germany.

ghetto—A blighted neighborhood where Jews were forced to live during World War II.

interrogate—To question officially and often intensively.

judenrein—Free of Jews (German).

liquidate—The word used by Nazis to mean the closing or destruction of a ghetto. Ghetto residents were often shipped to death camps.

FURTHER READING

Appleman-Jurman, Alicia. *Alicia: My Story*. New York: Bantam Books, 1990.

Bacon, Ursula. *Shanghai Diary*. Milwaukie, Ore.: M Press, 2004.

Buergenthal, Thomas. *A Lucky Child: A Memoir of Surviving Auschwitz as a Young Boy*. New York: Little, Brown and Company, 2009.

Fox, Anne and Eva Abraham-Podietz. *Ten Thousand Children: True Stories Told by Children Who Escaped the Holocaust on the Kindertransport*. West Orange, N.J.: Behrman House, 1999.

Harris, Mark Jonathan and Deborah Oppenheimer. *Into the Arms of Strangers: Stories of the Kindertransport*. New York: Bloomsbury USA, 2001.

Smith, Lyn. *Remembering: Voices of the Holocaust: A New History in the Words of the Men and Women Who Survived*. New York: Carol & Graf, 2006.

Turner, Barry. *One Small Suitcase*. London: Puffin Books, 2003.

INTERNET ADDRESSES

The Kindertransport Association
   <http://www.kindertransport.org/>

Voyage of the *St. Louis*—
   United States Holocaust Memorial Museum
   <http://www.ushmm.org/museum/exhibit/online/stlouis/>

Yad Vashem: The Holocaust Martyrs' and
   Heroes' Remembrance Authority
   <http://www.yadvashem.org/>

INDEX

A

Auschwitz, 61, 75, 109
Austria, 37–39, 51, 84, 105

B

Bacon, Ursula, 31–33
Baran, Sally, 75–77
Belgium, 25, 51, 68, 70, 71
Belzec, 102
Benitez, Manuel, 63
Berkowicz, Ruth, 79–81, 87–89
Betar, 45–47
Blachmann, Gerda, 66–68
blitzkreig, 23, 25, 71, 95
Buczacz, Poland, 7–9, 11–12, 14
Buergenthal, Thomas, 113–114

C

China, 33, 87–89
Cohn, Paul, 56–57
concentration camps, 19–22, 50,
    81, 100. See also specific camps.
Cuba, 63, 66
Czechoslovakia, 38, 41, 51, 57–61

D

Dachau, 22, 50, 110
death camps, 8, 44, 95, 102, 108,
    111
death marches, 109–111, 114
deportations, 57, 60–61, 75, 81, 82,
    100, 102

E

Ebostarkova, Alice, 52–53, 57–61

Eckstut, Erika, 91–93
Ederer, Fred, 19–22
Einsatzgruppen (death or killing
    squads), 9–10, 14–15, 75–77
Eisen, Renata, 99–100
England. See Great Britain.

F

families
    reunification of, 35–37, 79–81,
        100
    separation of, 29–30, 35, 37,
        42–44, 52–53, 65, 89
Feldman, Alfred, 71–75
Feldman, Gerda, 22–23, 63–66,
    68–70
"final solution," 95, 115
France
    as destination, 37, 41–44, 62,
        71–73
    expulsion of Jews by, 84
    limitations on refugees by, 23
    occupation of, 27, 42, 68, 70,
        71

G

Galler, Eva, 102–105
Gerechter, Johanna, 89–91
ghettos
    Buczacz, 7–9
    in China, 87
    establishment of, 27
    food, smuggling into, 91–93,
        99
    liquidation of, 8–9, 106
Gittelman, Florence, 77–78

Great Britain
  as desirable destination, 68–70
  Kindertransport program.
    See Kindertransport program.
  limitations on refugees by, 23
  Nazi failure in, 70

H

Hitler, Adolf, 16, 23, 38, 40, 81, 95, 109
Holland (Netherlands), 27, 51, 68, 70, 71
hunger, 11, 110

I

identities, false, 11–12, 73
informers, 76–77, 102
Italy, 33, 89–91, 99–100
Itzkowitz, Sam, 110–111

J

Japan, 36, 46–48, 87–89
Jewish Fighting Organization (ZOB), 105–108
Jewish people, impoverishment of, 16–19, 50
Jurman, Alicia, 7–15
Jurman, Zachary, 7, 8

K

Kindertransport program
  accounts of, 52–63
  adapting, difficulties with, 62–63
  establishment of, 50
  funding, 50–51
  mechanics of, 51–52
  memory, difficulties with, 57–62

Konrad, Evelyn, 42–44, 84–86
Kovner, Abba, 95–99
Kristallnacht, 19–23, 50

L

labor camps, 73, 76–77, 97, 105
Lithuania, 44, 87, 95, 97
luck, importance of, 111–115

M

Melamed, Leo, 33–37

N

Nazi brutality
  beatings, 17, 32
  forced labor, 73, 77, 105
  murders, 7–10, 14–15, 29, 37, 75–78
  population control, 33–35
  theft, 32, 82
Norway, 25, 71, 81–84
Nuremberg Laws, 16–19

O

Operation Barbarossa, 95

P

Perlmutter, Shulamit, 27–30
Poland, invasion of, 23–27
Ponary, 97
Portugal, 42, 84
psychological effects
  adaptation difficulties, 62–63, 94
  depression, 81–82
  family separations, 29–30, 35, 37, 42–44, 52–53, 65
  memory difficulties, 57–62

of Nazi brutality, 12–14, 33, 36
refusal of asylum, 66–70
survivor guilt, 107–108, 114

R

Rappoport, Eva, 37
refuge
 refusal of, 77, 78
 safe houses, 8, 12, 27, 73
 searching for, 31–33
refugees
 acceptance of, 22–25, 50
 assistance for, 89–91
 children, rescue of, 50–63
 dangers of being, 71
 penalty for helping, 94
 psychological effects on.
  See psychological effects.
 refusal of, 66–70, 77, 78, 100
 survival instincts, importance
  of, 44–49, 77–81, 100
Reif-Lehrer, Liane, 17–19
Roosevelt, Franklin D., 66
Rosenberg, Margrit, 81–84
Rotem, Simha, 24–25, 106–107

S

Sachs, Inge, 61–63
Schenker, Alexander, 111–113
Schleissner, Edith, 38–42
smuggling, 91–93, 99
Sondheimer, Hanni, 87–89

Soviet Union, 12, 23–25, 75, 89,
 95, 109, 114
St. Louis, 50, 63–70
Sugihara, Chiune, 47–49
Sweden, 83–84
Switzerland, 100, 110
Szepsenwol, Chaya, Feiga, 45–49

T

Treblinka, 44

U

U-boats, 86
United Partisans Organization
 (FPO), 95–99
United States
 acceptance of refugees by, 15,
  42, 43, 86
 as destination, 20, 22, 36
 limitations on refugees by, 23
 refusal of refugees by, 66, 68

W

waiting, risks of, 38–42
Warsaw Ghetto uprising, 105–108
Weintraub, Roza, 44–45, 93–94
Weiss, Fritzie, 109–110
Wellen, Einar, 82, 83
Wollheim, Norbert, 54–56

Z

Zuckerman, Yitzhak, 25